Alger Hiss and the Rosenbergs: The Spies at the Hei

By Charles River Editors

A picture of Alger Hiss testifying

About Charles River Editors

Charles River Editors provides superior editing and original writing services across the digital publishing industry, with the expertise to create digital content for publishers across a vast range of subject matter. In addition to providing original digital content for third party publishers, we also republish civilization's greatest literary works, bringing them to new generations of readers via ebooks.

Sign up here to receive updates about free books as we publish them, and visit Our Kindle Author Page to browse today's free promotions and our most recently published Kindle titles.

Introduction

Alger Hiss

"I am amazed; until the day I die I shall wonder how Whittaker Chambers got into my house to use my typewriter." – Alger Hiss

"We won the Hiss case in the papers. We did. I had to leak stuff all over the place. Because the Justice Department would not prosecute it. Hoover didn't even cooperate.... It was won in the papers. I leaked out the papers.... I leaked out the testimony. I had Hiss convicted before he ever got to the grand jury.... Go back and read the chapter on the Hiss case in Six Crises and you'll see how it was done. It wasn't done waiting for the goddamn courts or the attorney general or the FBI." – Richard Nixon

Shortly after World War II, Congress' House Committee on Un-American Activities began investigating Americans across the country for suspected ties to Communism. The most famous victims of these witch hunts were Hollywood actors, such as Charlie Chaplin, whose "Un-American activity" was being neutral at the beginning of World War II, but at the beginning of the Cold War, many Americans had the Red Scare, and Wisconsin Senator Joseph McCarthy would make waves in 1950 by telling the Republican Women's Club in Wheeling, West Virginia that he had a list of dozens of known Communists working in the State Department. The political theater helped Senator McCarthy become the prominent anti-Communist crusader in the government, and McCarthy continued to claim he held evidence suggesting Communist infiltration throughout the government, but anytime he was pressed to produce his evidence, McCarthy would not name names. Instead, he'd accuse those who questioned his evidence of being Communists themselves.

Among the people called before the House Committee on Un-American Activities, none are as controversial as Alger Hiss. Hiss had graduated from Harvard Law, after which he worked as a clerk for Supreme Court Justice Oliver Wendell Holmes, worked in the Roosevelt administration for the Agricultural Adjustment Association, and was Head of the Carnegie Endowment for International Peace. That background didn't exactly sound like one held by a Soviet spy, let alone a Communist, but Elizabeth Bentley, a former Communist, notified the Committee about a suspected spy ring and named several names, including Hiss. More notably, Hiss was also accused of being a Communist and Soviet spy by an admitted Communist, Whittaker Chambers.

The Hiss case came at a time when the Committee was populated by right-wing zealots, including a young Congressman from California named Richard Nixon. Decorum was in scarce supply, and "Hiss was everything Nixon despised...wealthy, liberal, educated and handsome." Although Hiss was believed at first and Nixon was cast as the public villain for doggedly questioning him over Communist ties, Chambers eventually produced State Department documents typed on Hiss's typewriter, and Hiss was forced to admit that he previously knew and had associated with Chambers, who had renounced his Communism and had become editor of *Time Magazine*. Though the FBI and the Committee were never able to prove Hiss was a spy, they were able to get Hiss on a charge of perjury, for which he was sentenced to five years in prison, and the conviction of Hiss added to the luster of Nixon's anti-communist credentials.

To this day, controversy still swirls over whether Hiss was actually a Soviet spy. Hiss claimed he was innocent of the charges his entire life, but the authors of *Spies: The Rise and Fall of the KGB in America* strongly assert Hiss was actually a spy, writing that "continued claims for Hiss's innocence are akin to a terminal case of ideological blindness." Military historian Eduard Mark wrote that the evidence "conclusively show[s] that Hiss was, as Whittaker Chambers charged more than six decades ago, an agent of Soviet military intelligence (GRU) in the 1930s." Conversely, others have cited lack of hard evidence and available Soviet documents to make definitive conclusions.

Alger Hiss and the Rosenbergs: The Controversial Trials of the Alleged Soviet Spies at the Height of the Red Scare chronicles the controversial history of the Alger Hiss case and the debate over whether he was a Soviet spy. Along with pictures of important people, places, and events, you will learn about Hiss like never before.

The Rosenbergs

"I consider your crime worse than murder...I believe your conduct in putting into the hands of the Russians the A-Bomb years before our best scientists predicted Russia would perfect the bomb has already caused, in my opinion, the Communist aggression in Korea, with the resultant casualties exceeding 50,000 and who knows but that millions more of innocent people may pay the price of your treason. Indeed, by your betrayal you undoubtedly have altered the course of history to the disadvantage of our country. No one can say that we do not live in a constant state of tension. We have evidence of your treachery all around us every day for the civilian defense activities throughout the nation are aimed at preparing us for an atom bomb attack." – Judge Irving Kaufman

"This death sentence is not surprising. It had to be. There had to be a Rosenberg case, because there had to be an intensification of the hysteria in America to make the Korean War acceptable to the American people. There had to be hysteria and a fear sent through America in order to get increased war budgets. And there had to be a dagger thrust in the heart of the left to tell them that you are no longer gonna get five years for a Smith Act prosecution or one year for contempt of court, but we're gonna kill ya!" – Julius Rosenberg

In 1947, President Truman had tried to assure Americans, "I am not worried about the Communist Party taking over the Government of the United States, but I am against a person, whose loyalty is not to the Government of the United States, holding a Government job. They are entirely different things. I am not worried about this country ever going Communist. We have too much sense for that." Nonetheless, shortly after World War II, Congress' House Committee on Un-American Activities began investigating Americans across the country for suspected ties to Communism.

However, the case of Alger Hiss and the rise of McCarthyism were undoubtedly instrumental in the way that one of the most notorious cases in American history unfolded in the early 1950s. After years of keeping tabs on Julius and Ethel Rosenberg, the two Communist sympathizers were indicted on charges of treason and conspiracy to commit espionage for passing off secrets about the atomic bomb to the Soviet Union.

In the context of the Cold War and the Korean War, there could hardly be more serious charges, but the couple strenuously asserted their innocence, even after they were implicated by Ethel's own brother, David Greenglass. Throughout the trial and its aftermath, many Americans believed the Rosenbergs were innocent and/or were facing an unduly harsh death sentence. Indeed, authorities had hoped to wring confessions out of the two by threatening them with the chair, but they held steadfast all the way up until their executions on June 19, 1953.

In the over 60 years since, there has been plenty of debate over whether the two of them were guilty, and, if so, what the extent of their espionage was. While historians have used declassified documents and memoirs of involved individuals to reach the widespread belief that Julius Rosenberg did commit espionage, there is still a lot of doubt regarding Ethel's involvement, and scholars still debate just what Julius may have sent the Soviets. The mystery and intrigue still surrounding the case, trial, and executions continue to fascinate people and generate plenty of ongoing speculation.

Alger Hiss and the Rosenbergs: The Controversial Trials of the Alleged Soviet Spies at the Height of the Red Scare chronicles the events that led to the infamous trial and execution of the Rosenbergs. Along with pictures of important people, places, and events, you will learn about the Rosenbergs like never before.

Alger Hiss and the Rosenbergs: The Controversial Trials of the Alleged Soviet Spies at the Height of the Red Scare

About Charles River Editors

Introduction

Chapter 1: I Did Not Wish to Testify

Chapter 2: The Extent of the Communist Infiltration

Chapter 3: A Trapped Man

Chapter 4: The Incident of the Pumpkin

Chapter 5: The Hiss Case

Chapter 6: Waiting for the Returns to Come In

Chapter 7: Opened Files

Chapter 8: A Practiced Hand

Chapter 9: According to Ruth Greenglass

Chapter 10: Rosenberg Responded

Chapter 11: Tangible and Circumstantial Evidence

Online Resources

Bibliography

Chapter 1: I Did Not Wish to Testify

"I did not wish to testify before the House Committee. I prayed that, if it were God's will, I might be spared that ordeal. ... The things that I had to tell were ten years old and I had only to let the shadows, dust and cobwebs conspicuously drape them to leave the stand unscathed. I could not do it. I believed that I was not meant to be spared from testifying. I sensed, with a force greater than any fear or revulsion, that it was for this that my whole life had been lived. For this I had been a Communist, for this I had ceased to be a Communist. For this the tranquil strengthening years had been granted to me. This challenge was the terrible meaning of my whole life, of all that I had done that was evil, of all that I had sought that was good, of my weakness and my strength. Everything that made me peculiarly myself, and different from all others, qualified me to testify. My failure to do so, any attempt to evade that necessity, would be a betrayal that would measure nothing less than the destruction of my own soul. I felt this beyond any possibility of avoiding it." - Whittaker Chambers, *Witness*

In the wake of World War II, the European continent was devastated, leaving the Soviet Union and the United States as uncontested superpowers. This ushered in over 45 years of the Cold War, and a political alignment of Western democracies against the Communist Soviet bloc that literally split Berlin in two. In addition to dividing Berlin, the Soviet Union and its allies, and the United States and its allies competed for influence and attempted to undermine each other's geopolitical power. Due to the devastating nuclear weapons both sides possessed, both sides attempted to avoid fighting each other for fear that any skirmish could escalate into a full nuclear war, but that didn't stop all conflicts. Instead, the competition bubbled up in diplomatic confrontations, proxy wars, arms races and general rivalry between the nations.

The Cold War was so named because, even though the United States and the Soviet Union were adversaries across the globe, major fighting between the militaries of the two superpowers was avoided, so the war never got hot. At the same time, both sides had spy networks across the world working against each other, and with Americans looking to ferret out Communists in their midst, the nation was ripe for a scandal when Alger Hiss stepped onto the stage.

In many ways, Hiss was an unusual candidate for an espionage case at the height of the Red Scare during the mid-20th century. Hiss had been born into a comfortable, upper middle class family in Baltimore, Maryland, but he seemed plagued by misfortune from the very beginning of his life. His father, depressed over failed business dealings, committed suicide when little Alger was only two years old, and when he later learned the nature of his father's death, he became obsessed with restoring his family's honor. However, he was hampered in this by his older brother Bosley's illness and early death, as well as his older sister's suicide.

Despite these tragedies, Alger persevered, graduating first from Johns Hopkins University and then from Harvard Law School. He then clerked for Supreme Court Justice Oliver Wendell Holmes, Jr., subsequently joined the prominent Boston law firm Choate, Hall & Stewart, and finally moved to New York to work at Cotton, Franklin, Wright & Gordon.

Holmes and Hiss circa 1930

Politically liberal, Hiss soon found work in Franklin Roosevelt's administration, and this is when he began to make political enemies, first by defending the Agricultural Adjustment Administration against attempts by more conservative leaders to disband it and later by serving as an assistant to Assistant Secretary of State Francis B. Sayre. After those stints, he ended up in the Office of Far Eastern Affairs, where he served during the early years of World War II.

Sayre

In 1944, Hiss reached the pinnacle of his career when he became Director of the Office of Special Political Affairs, an organization created to help shape the postwar world. In this capacity, he was among those who began to work on creating the United Nations, and in 1945 he attended the Yalta Conference, where he helped assemble papers on "any general matters that might come up relating to the Far East or the Near East." After serving as secretary-general of the United Nations Conference on International Organization, he became president of the Carnegie Endowment for International Peace in 1946.

Hiss at a UN conference in 1946

Ultimately, Hiss' fall from grace began in the summer of 1948 when a former Communist named Whittaker Chambers appeared before the House Un-American Activities Committee (HUAC). Chambers later claimed that he had never wanted to appear before the committee but felt "the moment had arrived when some man must be a witness, and so had the man. They had come together. The danger to the nation from Communism had now grown acute, both within its own house and abroad. Its existence was threatened. And the nation did not know it. For the first time, the Committee's subpoena gave me an opportunity to tell what I knew about that danger, not for the special information and purposes of this or that security agency, however important its work. I knew that the F.B.I., for example, could not initiate action against Communism. By law it could only gather information which the Justice Department might, or might not act on, as it saw fit."

Chambers

On August 3, 1948, Chambers testified, "For a number of years I had myself served in the under-ground, chiefly in Washington, D. C. The heart of my report to the United States Government consisted of a description of the apparatus to which I was attached. It was an underground organization of the United States Communist Party developed, to the best of my knowledge, by Harold Ware... The head of the underground group at the time I knew it was Nathan Witt, an attorney for the National Labor Relations Board. Later, John Abt became the leader. Lee Pressman was also a member of this group, as was Alger Hiss, who, as a member of the State Department, later organized the conferences at Dumbarton Oaks, San Francisco, and the United States side of the Yalta Conference. The purpose of this group at that time was not primarily espionage. Its original purpose was the Communist infiltration of the American Government. But espionage was certainly one of its eventual objectives. ... The Communist Party exists for the specific purpose of overthrowing the Government; at the opportune time, by any and all means; and each of its members, by the fact that he is a member, is dedicated to this purpose."

Abt

Pressman

Witt

One of the things the Committee was interested in was whether Chambers had tried to convince anyone else to leave with him. Chambers told the Congressmen, "The only one of those people whom I approached was Alger Hiss. I went to the Hiss home one evening at what I considered considerable risk to myself and found Mrs. Hiss at home. Mrs. Hiss is also a member of the Communist Party. ... Mrs. Hiss attempted while I was there to make a call, which I can only presume was to other Communists, but I quickly went to the telephone and she hung up, and Mr. Hiss came in shortly afterward, and we talked and I tried to break him away from the party. As a matter of fact, he cried when we separated; when I left him, but he absolutely refused to break."

A picture of the Hiss home in the 1930s

When these allegations reached the press, Hiss quickly telegraphed Parnell Thomas, the chairman of the HUAC, with a categorical rejection of Chambers' testimony: "I do not know Mr. Chambers and, so far as I am aware, have never laid eyes on him. There is no basis for the statements about me made to your committee...I would further appreciate the opportunity of appearing before your committee..."

J. Parnell Thomas

Not surprisingly, the Committee welcomed Hiss to testify, which he did a couple of days later on August 5. Hiss said, "I was born in Baltimore. Md., on November 11, 1904. I am here at my own request to deny unqualifiedly various statements about me which were made before this committee by one Whittaker Chambers the day before yesterday. I appreciate the Committee's having promptly granted my request. I welcome the opportunity to answer to the best of my ability any inquiries the members of this committee may wish to ask me. I am not and never have been a member of the Communist Party. I do not and never have adhered to the tenets of the Communist Party. I am not and never have been a member of any Communist-front organization. I have never followed the Communist Party line, directly or indirectly. To the best of my knowledge, none of my friends is a Communist. As a State Department official, I have had contacts with representatives of foreign governments, some of whom have undoubtedly been members of the Communist Party, as, for example, representatives of the Soviet Government. My contacts with any foreign representative who could possibly have been a Communist have been strictly official. To the best of my knowledge, I never heard of Whittaker Chambers until in 1947, when two representatives of the Federal Bureau of Investigation asked me if I knew him and various other people, some of whom I knew and some of whom I did not know. I said I did not know Chambers. So far as I know, I have never laid eyes on him, and I should like to have the opportunity to do so."

Hiss admitted that he did know some of the men he was accused of interacting with, but he went out of his way to assure the Committee that any relationship he had with them was insignificant: "I have known Henry Collins since we were boys in camp together. I knew him again while he was at the Harvard Business School while I was at the Harvard Law School, and I have seen him from time to time since I came to Washington in 1933. Lee Pressman was in my class at the Harvard Law School and we were both on the Harvard Law Review at the same time. We were also both assistants to Judge Jerome Frank on the legal staff of the Agricultural Adjustment Administration. Since I left the Department of Agriculture I have seen him only occasionally and infrequently. I left the Department, according to my recollection, in 1935. Witt and Abt were both members of the legal staff of the AAA. I knew them both in that capacity. I believe I met Witt in New York a year or so before I came to Washington. I came to Washington in 1933. We were both practicing law in New York at the time I think I met Witt. Kramer was in another office of the AAA, and I met him in that connection. I have seen none of these last three men I have mentioned except most infrequently since I left the Department of Agriculture. I don't believe I ever knew Victor Perlo. Except as I have indicated, the statements made about me by Mr. Chambers are complete fabrications. I think my record in the Government service speaks for itself."

A picture of Hiss testifying at his first hearing

Chapter 2: The Extent of the Communist Infiltration

"I had already been warned by other sources - and was soon to be warned by the Committee - that the Justice Department was preparing to move against me, that it was actively making plans to indict me, and not Alger Hiss, for perjury on the basis of my testimony before the House Committee. I felt that my testimony had offended the powers that for so long had kept from the nation the extent of the Communist infiltration of Government, and the official heights to which it had reached. Not Alger Hiss (for denying any of the truth), but I (for revealing part of the truth) was to be punished. I became convinced then, and the immense mass of power that was tilted against me right up to the end of the first Hiss trial clinched my conviction, that the facts in the Hiss Case had come to light in the only way, time and place that they could have come to light. The very pressures that had made for their long suppression, once the facts reached the surface, contributed to the force with which, like a gusher, they burst out and filled the national landscape with a blackness malodorous and crude. I myself was only a chip in the play of that torrent." – Whittaker Chambers

Initially, Hiss' testimony completely convinced the Committee members that he was innocent, and it also convinced many Americans that the Committee itself was suspect. President Harry Truman even called the inquiry "a red herring to keep [the members of the committee] from doing what they ought to do." Indeed, throughout his presidency, Truman tried to play down public fears, and privately he despised McCarthy. In 1947, the president had tried to assure Americans, "I am not worried about the Communist Party taking over the Government of the United States, but I am against a person, whose loyalty is not to the Government of the United States, holding a Government job. They are entirely different things. I am not worried about this country ever going Communist. We have too much sense for that." Many years later, after the hysteria had waned, Truman thunderously asserted in 1960, "I've said many a time that I think the Un-American Activities Committee in the House of Representatives was the most un-American thing in America!"

Truman

However, one up-and-coming politician strongly disagreed with Truman's sentiment. Richard Nixon, then a Congressman from California, insisted that where there was smoke, there was fire, as he later wrote: "The conduct of President Truman in this case was particularly hard to understand. No one would question the tough-minded anti-Communism of [Truman].... One can understand why he might have felt justified in terming the case a 'red herring' when Hiss first testified before the Committee. But he did a disservice to the nation and to his own party by stubbornly maintaining that position as evidence to the contrary piled up. His error was sheer stubbornness in refusing to admit a mistake. He viewed the Hiss case only in its political implications and he chose to handle the crisis which faced his Administration with an outworn political rule of thumb: leave the political skeletons hidden in the closet and keep the door locked. He denied outright the evidence in front of him and he stumped the 1948 political trail flailing away at the 'red herring,' thus putting himself in a needlessly untenable position on an important issue and-of infinitely graver consequence- leading a large segment of the public away from a deeper understanding of the true threat of the Communist conspiracy in America."

Nixon in 1950

Nixon, Robert Stripling, and Thomas as members of the HUAC

Nixon also happened to be appointed as the chairman of a subcommittee assigned to determine which man was telling the truth between Chambers and Hiss, and on August 7, 1948, Nixon again questioned Chambers, this time looking for evidence that the he really did know Hiss as well as he claimed he did. For nearly three hours, Nixon peppered Chambers with questions about the details of Hiss' life, details only a friend would know. Chambers recalled, "As nearly as I can remember, [the Hisses] had a maid who came in to clean and a cook who came in to cook. I can't remember whether they had a maid there all the time or not. It seems to me in one or two of the houses they did. In one of the houses they had a rather elderly Negro maid whom Mr. Hiss used to drive home in the evening. ... Hiss is a man of great simplicity and a great gentleness and sweetness of character, and they lived with extreme simplicity. I had the impression that the furniture in that house was kind of pulled together from here or there, maybe got it from their mother or something like that, nothing lavish about it whatsoever, quite simple. Their food was in the same pattern and they cared nothing about food. It was not a primary interest in their lives. ... They both had the same hobby amateur ornithologists, bird observers. They used to get up early in the morning and go to Glen Echo, out the canal, to observe birds. I recall once they saw, to their great excitement, a prothonotary warbler."

It was this last detail that proved to be critical, as it was such a fine point that it seemed no one outside Hiss' inner circle would know about it.

Then there was the matter of the Hiss car, about which Chambers shared an interesting detail: "When I first knew them they had a car. ... I remember very clearly that it had hand windshield wipers. I remember that because I drove it one rainy day and had to work those windshield wipers by hand. ... The Communist Party had in Washington a service station-that is, the man in charge or owner of this station was a Communist-or it may have been a car lot. The owner was a Communist. ... It was against all the rules of underground organization for Hiss to do anything with his old car but trade it in...but Hiss insisted that he wanted that car turned over to the open party so it could be of use to some poor organizer in the West or somewhere. Much against my better judgment and much against Peters' better judgment, he finally got us to permit him to do this thing. Peters knew where this lot was and he either took Hiss there, or he gave Hiss the address and Hiss went there, and to the best of my recollection of his description of that happening, he left the car there and simply went away and the man in charge of the station took care of the rest of it for him."

The subcommittee also questioned Chambers about the role of Hiss' brother, who he also claimed was a Communist. Chambers answered, "Donald Hiss was married, I think to a daughter of Mr. Cotton, who is in the State Department. She was not a Communist, and everybody was worried about her. ... [Donald Hiss] was much less intelligent than Alger. Much less sensitive than his brother. I had the impression he was interested in the social climb and the Communist Party was interested in having him climb. At one point I believe he was fairly friendly with James Roosevelt. ... He was working in the Labor Department, I believe in the Immigration Section, and it was the plan of the Communist Party to have him go to California, get himself sent by the Government to California, to work on the Bridges case. At that moment he had an opportunity to go into the State Department as, I think, legal adviser to the Philippine Section, which had just been set up. It was the opinion of the party that he should do that and not the Bridges matter. It was his opinion that he should continue in the Bridges matter and there was a fairly sharp exchange, but he submitted to discipline and went to the State Department."

Within days, Donald Hiss railed against Chambers' accusations that he was a Communist, insisting, "I flatly deny every statement made by Mr. Chambers with respect to me. I am not, and never have been, a member of the Communist Party or of any formal or informal organizations affiliated with, or fronting in any manner whatsoever for, the Communist Party. In fact, the only organizations and clubs to which I have belonged are the local Y.M.C.A., the Miles River Yacht Club of Maryland, the old Washington Racquet Club, the Harvard Law School Association, the American Society of International Law, and college fraternities and athletic clubs. I have no recollection of ever having met any person by the name of D. Whittaker Chambers, nor do I recognize his photograph which I have seen in the public press. I am not and never have been in sympathy with the principles of the Communist Party ... I have never known that man by the name of Chambers, Carl, or any other name...If I am lying, I should go to jail, and if Mr. Chambers is lying, he should go to jail."

Donald Hiss

Nonetheless, with this information in hand, the Committee called on Hiss to appear again, this time before an executive session on August 16. In speaking to Hiss, Committee Investigator Robert Stripling observed pointedly, "I listened to his testimony in New York.... He sat there and testified for hours. He said he spent a week in your house and he just rattled off details like that. He has either made a study of your life in great detail or he knows you, one or the other, or he is incorrect." Committee Chairman J. Parnell Thomas then showed Hiss two different photographs of Chambers, but Hiss remained adamant about not knowing him: "I have never known anyone who had the relationship with me that this man has testified to and that, I think, is the important thing here, gentlemen. This man may have known me, he may have been in my house. I have had literally hundreds of people in my house in the course of the time I lived in Washington. The issue is not whether this man knew me and I don't remember him. The issue is whether he had a particular conversation that he has said he had with me and which I have denied and whether I am a member of the Communist Party or ever was, which he has said and which I have denied. If I could see the man face to face, I would perhaps have some inkling as to whether he ever had known me personally."

Hiss then introduced the possibility that Chambers could have gotten his detailed information about the interior of his family home from "a man named George Crosley." Hiss went on to explain, "He was a writer. He hoped to sell articles to magazines about the munitions industry. … This fellow was writing a series of articles…which he hoped to sell to one of the magazines. He was pretty obviously not successful in financial terms, but as far as I know, wasn't actually hard up. ... After we had taken the house on P Street and had the apartment on our hands, he one day in the course of casual conversation said he was going to specialize all summer in getting his articles done here in Washington, didn't know what he was going to do, and was thinking of bringing his family. I said, 'You can have my apartment. It is not terribly cool, but it is up in the air near the Wardman Park.' ...he spent several nights in my house because his furniture van was delayed. ... The P Street house belonged to a naval officer overseas and was partly furnished, so we didn't need all our furniture, particularly during the summer months, and...we left several pieces of furniture behind until the fall, his van was delayed, wasn't going to bring all the furniture because he was going to be there just during the summer, and we put them up 2 or 3 nights in a row.... [He had] Very bad teeth. That is one of the things I particularly want to see Chambers about. This man had very bad teeth, did not take care of his teeth. I don't think he had gapped teeth, but they were badly taken care of. They were stained and I would say obviously not attended to."

There was, however, still the matter of Hiss' bird watching, a hobby that proved to be Nixon's ace in the hole. The following exchange took place during the afternoon session:

Mr. NIXON. What hobby, if any, do you have, Mr. Hiss?
Mr. HISS. Tennis and amateur ornithology.
Mr. NIXON. Is your wife interested in ornithology?
Mr. HISS. I also like to swim and also like to sail. My wife is interested in ornithology, as I am, through my interest. Maybe I am using too big a word to say an ornithologist because I am pretty amateur, but I have been interested in it since I was in Boston. I think anybody who knows me would know that.
Mr. McDOWELL. Did you ever see a prothonotary warbler?
Mr. HISS. I have right here on the Potomac. Do you know that place?
The CHAIRMAN. What is that?
Mr. NIXON. Have you ever seen one?
Mr. HISS. Did you see it in the same place?
Mr. McDOWELL. I saw one in Arlington.
Mr. HISS. They come back and nest in those swamps. Beautiful yellow head, a gorgeous bird. Mr. Collins is an ornithologist, Henry Collins. He is a really good ornithologist, calling them by their Latin names.

This testimony proved to be the start of Hiss' undoing because nobody on the Committee believed that anyone could have known such a detail about Henry Collins without being at least intimately associated with him. This was especially damaging since Chambers had testified on August 3 that Collins was the treasurer of the Communist group that Hiss belonged to, and that it was Collins who collected the dues from members before giving it over to Chambers.

Chapter 3: A Trapped Man

"Until we faced each other in the hotel room, I had been testifying about Hiss as a memory and a name. Now I saw again the man himself. In the circumstances it was shocking. Until then, I had wondered how he could be so arrogant or so stupid as to suppose that he could deceive the nation into believing that he had never known me. (I did not know that Hiss had already tentatively identified me, with infinite qualification, as George Crosley.) But when I saw him in person, that feeling, too, fell away, and I was swept by a sense of pity for all trapped men of which the pathos of this man was the center. For the man I saw before me was a trapped man. Under the calculated malice of his behavior toward me, which I could not fail to resent, under his impudence and bravado to the congressmen, he was a trapped man— and I am a killer only by extreme necessity. Throughout the session, my mind was in a posture of supplication, silently imploring strength for him to disclose the truth that I had already testified to about him so that I might not be compelled to testify to worse about him and the others." – Whittaker Chambers

The stage was now set for a showdown the next day, during which the two men came face to face for the first time since the whole affair started in the hotel room where the hearings were being held. While Chambers was stating his name, Hiss approached him and all but identified him as the same George Crosley he had mentioned in his testimony on August 16. This led to the following exchange:

> Mr. HISS. Would you mind opening your mouth wider?
> Mr. CHAMBERS. My name is Whittaker Chambers.
> Mr. HISS. I said, would you open your mouth? You know what I am referring to, Mr. Nixon. Will you go on talking?
> Mr. CHAMBERS. I am senior editor of Time magazine.
> Mr. HISS. May I ask whether his voice, when he testified before was comparable to this?
> Mr. NIXON. His voice?
> Mr. HISS. Or did he talk a little more in a lower key?
> Mr. McDOWELL. I would say it is about the same now as we have heard.
> Mr. HISS. Would you ask him to talk a little more?
> Mr. NIXON. Read something, Mr. Chambers. I will let you read from- .
> Mr. HISS. I think he is George Crosley, but I would like to hear him talk a little longer.
> Mr. McDOWELL. Mr. Chambers, if you would be more comfortable, you may sit down.
> Mr. HISS. Are you George Crosley?
> Mr. CHAMBERS. Not to my knowledge. You are Alger Hiss, I believe.
> Mr. HISS. I certainly am.
> Mr. CHAMBERS. That was my recollection.

Hiss continued to stare at Chambers as Nixon questioned him, finally coming to the matter of his teeth.

Mr. HISS. The voice sounds a little less resonant than the voice than I recall of the man I knew as George Crosley. The teeth look to me as though either they have been improved upon or that there has been considerable dental work done since I knew George Crosley, which was some years ago. I believe I am not prepared without further checking to take an absolute oath that he must be George Crosley.

...

Mr. NIXON. Mr. Chambers, have you had any dental work since 1934 of a substantial nature?

Mr. CHAMBERS. Yes; I have.

Mr. NIXON. What type of dental work?

Mr. CHAMBERS. I have had some extractions and a plate.

Mr. NIXON. Have you had any dental work in the front of your mouth?

Mr. CHAMBERS. Yes.

Mr. NIXON. What is the nature of that work?

Mr. CHAMBERS. That is a plate in place of some of the upper dentures.

Mr. NIXON. I see.

...

Mr. HISS. I would like a few more questions asked. I didn't intend to say anything about this, because I feel very strongly that he is Crosley, but he looks very different in girth and in other appearances-hair, forehead. And so on, particularly the jowls.

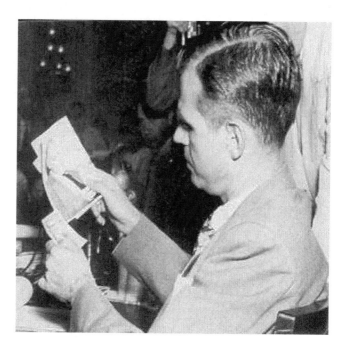

A picture of Hiss examining a picture of Chambers

After the questions, Hiss testified that he believed Chambers to be the man he had previously known as George Crosley, but this did not end his problems. Stripling asked, "Will you produce for the committee three people who will testify that they knew him as George Crosley?" This angered Hiss, who replied, "I will if it is possible. Why is that a question to ask me? I will see what is possible. This occurred in 1935. The only people that I can think of who could have known him as George Crosley with certainty would have been the people who were associated with me in the Nye committee. ... I am afraid I will have to confer with the individual members. The people, as I recall them, who were on that staff - and they were in and out of Washington constantly - were Mr. Raushenbush. I would like to consult Steve Raushenbush. I don't know whether Crosley ever called on him...."

Then, Nixon asked, "Will you tell the committee whether or not during this period of time that you knew him, which included periods of 3 nights or 2 or 3 nights, in which he stayed overnight and one trip to New York, from any conversation you ever had any idea that he might be a Communist?" This made Hiss even angrier: "I certainly didn't...May I just state for the record that it was not the habit in Washington in those days, when particularly if a member of the press called on you, to ask him before you had further conversation whether or not he was a Communist. It was a quite different atmosphere in Washington then than today. I had no reason to suspect George Crosley of being a Communist. It never occurred to me that he might be or whether that was of any significance to me if he was. He was a press representative and it was my duty to give him information, as I did any other member of the press. It was to the interest of the committee investigating the munitions industry, as its members and we of its staff saw it, to furnish guidance and information to people who were popularizing and writing about its work. I would like to say that to come here and discover that the ass under the lion's skin is Crosley. I don't know why your committee didn't pursue this careful method of interrogation at an earlier date before all the publicity. You told me yesterday you didn't know he was going to mention my name, although a lot of people now tell me that the press did know it in advance. They were apparently more effective in getting information than the committee itself. That is all I have to say now."

The problem was, of course, that he did have more to say. After Chambers again identified him as a Communist, Hiss became livid, rushing toward Chambers and crying out, "May I say for the record at this point, that I would like to invite Mr. Whittaker Chambers to make those same statements out of the presence of this committee without their being privileged for suit for libel. I challenge you to do it, and I hope you will do it damned quickly." When Russell asked him to sit down, Hiss refused and insisted, "I will sit down when the chairman asks me. Mr. Russell, when the chairman asks me to sit down."

At that point, the committee took a brief recess. However, things were just as contentious when the men returned. Chambers later recalled, "During the remainder of the hearing, Robert Stripling made the telling point. 'I am concerned,' he said to Hiss, 'with the statement you made before the Committee of Congress in the presence of quite a few hundred people that you didn't even know this person. You led the public and the press to believe that you didn't know such a person.' ... Thus, a fortnight after the Case began, Alger Hiss, by an operation itself a good deal like a dental extraction, was brought to admit that, indeed, he knew me perfectly well. The hearing closed with a decision to hold a public confrontation in Washington on August 25th. Subpoenas were issued to Hiss and me at once."

Chambers also later claimed that he dreaded the second confrontation and tried to get out of it: "I asked Nixon why there had to be a public hearing at all now that Hiss had admitted that he knew me. But if another hearing had to be held, why must it be public, why could it not be held in executive session? Patiently, he put me off with reasons that did not seem to me to make sense. When I became insistent, he said reluctantly, 'It is for your own sake that the Committee is holding a public hearing. The Department of Justice is all set to move in on you in order to save Hiss. They are planning to indict you at once. The only way to head them off is to let the public judge for itself which one of you is telling the truth. That is your only chance. That is why the hearing must be public.' 'If there is anything else that you have not told us about Hiss,' he added, 'now is the time to tell us. Think hard about it. If there is anything else, for your own sake, tell us now.'"

The hearings held on August 25 before the HUAC were made even more dramatic by the fact that they were televised. The Committee was well prepared and quickly began peppering Hiss with questions about why he loaned Chambers (Crosley) his apartment and car given that Hiss claimed he was practically a stranger. Aggravated with what he perceived to be Hiss' grandstanding, Congressman Felix Hebert finally interrupted him and said, "Wait just a minute. I will let you make all the speeches you want. Let me get mine in now. I repeat you are a very agile young man and a very clever young man and your conduct on all appearances before this committee has shown that you are very self-possessed and you know what you are doing and you know yourself why you are answering and how you are answering. Now, that is the reason why I am trying to find out exactly where the truth lies. I can't understand and I can't reconcile and resolve the situation that an individual of your intellect and your ability who gives to casual people his apartment, who tosses in an automobile, who doesn't know the laws of liability, who lends money to an individual just casually, is so cautious another time. It seems to me it is a demonstration of a very remarkable ability. No, that is the reason why I want to be sure in repeatedly asking these questions that there can be no doubt in anybody's mind about what you mean to say as contrasted to what you say."

A portrait of Hebert

Later that afternoon, Chambers again spoke again of Hiss' desire to donate his car to a good cause: "Mr. Hiss was a devoted and at that time a rather romantic Communist...The story has spread that in testifying against Mr. Hiss I am working out some old grudge, or motives of revenge or hatred. I do not hate Mr. Hiss. We were close friends, but we are caught in a tragedy of history. Mr. Hiss represents the concealed enemy against which we are all fighting, and I am fighting. I have testified against him with remorse and pity, but in a moment of history in which this Nation now stands, so help me God, I could not do otherwise. I had been to what I considered to be the proper governmental authorities at a much earlier date, and I had been in connection with them on more than one occasion and more than one agency. I could scarcely wish to jeopardize the position which I had gained among the good men by such an appearance as this. Nevertheless, I had long supposed it would come and I decided that when it came I would take the opportunity to act as I should."

Pictures of Hiss testifying

Picture of Chambers testifying

Chapter 4: The Incident of the Pumpkin

"Toward the end of August 1948, I finally found the strength to cross the bridge and enter that region of grief, fear and death beyond. There followed about one hundred days in which was largely determined the form that the Hiss Case would take, and even whether there would be a Hiss Case, as we know it, at all. No period of the Case, I think, is more perplexing to most people. That is not strange, for many unusual factors were present And there was going on a struggle in the dark between the forces which sought to bring the Hiss Case to light and those which opposed them. It is still impossible to be explicit about that struggle, in part because the full facts about the forces that, until the end, favored Alger Hiss, cannot in the nature of their operation be known. …I claim no infallibility for my views which freely stand subject to the light of clarifying facts— facts, not arguments. I can only describe that struggle as I experienced it in terms of what I then felt. The struggle imposed upon the acts which shaped it forms which seem strange, and to some, grotesque, for example, the incident of the pumpkin." – Whittaker Chambers

On August 27, 1948, the HUAC issued its report, which criticized Hiss for being "vague and evasive" and praised Chambers for being "forthright and emphatic." After reading the report, Hiss responded with a lengthy letter in which he accused the HUAC of "using the great powers and prestige of the United States Congress to help sworn traitors to besmirch any American they may pick upon."

That same evening, Chambers appeared on the radio show *Meet the Press*, and he later wrote about his appearance: "The question that we were met to ask and answer was put almost at once. Folliard put it: Are you willing to repeat your charge that Alger Hiss was a Communist? … I answered: 'Alger Hiss was a Communist and may still be one.' It was almost certainly the most important answer that I shall be called upon to give in my life— and not only for myself. Millions who heard, or heard of it, caught only its surface meaning: Whittaker Chambers had deliberately opened himself to a libel suit by Alger Hiss. … Of the mayhem that followed, only one question and answer seems worth remembering. It bears directly on the Hiss Case. I was asked something about the economic problem of Communism. I answered, citing Dostoyevsky: 'The problem of Communism is not an economic problem. The problem of Communism is the problem of atheism.' Tom Reynolds was the most unsparing of my questioners. His manner and bias are fixed, I think in one question. 'Do you find it easier,' he asked me, 'to make a living now than when you were in the Communist Party?' At the time, I was too busy answering to catch the inner animus of that and other sallies."

Folliard

A little over a month later, on October 8, Hiss filed the anticipated suit, and his attorneys also began an extensive investigation into Chambers' past. During a deposition, Hiss' attorney, William Marbury, demanded that Chambers turn over to the court "any correspondence, either typewritten or in handwriting from any member of the Hiss family." Ironically, this proved to be his own client's undoing, because Chambers had many such papers, including one of the most controversial and debated letters of the era. In a tale reminiscent of the spy novels of the era, Chambers explained, "I communicated with my wife's nephew, Nathan Levine, merely telling him that I was going to New York and asking him if he would have 'my things' ready for me. … 'My things,' he told me, were at his mother's house— my wife's sister's. … He led me to a bathroom, where, over the tub, a small window opened into a dumbwaiter shaft that had long been out of use. Inside the shaft was some kind of small shelf or ledge. There Levine had laid 'my things.' He climbed upon the tub, opened the little window and half disappeared into the shaft. When he reappeared, he handed me an envelope that was big, plump and densely covered with the clotted cobwebs and dust of a decade. As I took it from his hands, that accumulation slid to the floor. In surprise, for I had supposed that the envelope was a small one, I carried it to the kitchen, which was at the end of the hall, and laid it on a white enamel table top. …I opened the envelope and drew part way out the thick batch of copied State Department documents. At a glance, I saw that, besides those documents, and Hiss's handwritten memos, there were three cylinders of microfilm and a little spool of developed film (actually two strips). By a reflex of amazement, I pushed the papers back into the envelope. ... 'Good God,' I said, 'I did not know that this still existed.'"

Chambers immediately contacted his attorney and turned the documents over, but he withheld the film, not knowing exactly what was on it. On November 17, Marbury received the documents he had asked for but had not even thought existed. Chambers later recalled, "When the examination opened, I said that I should like to make a statement. I said, in substance, that until that time I had testified only to Alger Hiss's Communism. I had done so because I wished to shield him. I could not shield him completely, but I had hoped to shield him from the most shattering consequences of his acts as a Communist. I had tried to shield him because, in my own break with Communism, I had been given strength and a time in which to reshape my life. I did not wish to deprive Hiss and others of the same possibility that had been granted me. But now I must testify that Alger Hiss had also committed espionage. In response to William Marbury's request, I had brought evidence of that. Then I exposed the documents and the memos on the table in front of me."

In all, there were 65 documents, consisting of retyped State Department documents and four pages of State Department cables that had been copied out in Hiss' own handwriting. Chambers had hid the microfilm in a hollowed out pumpkin lying in the pumpkin patch at his family's farm in Westminster, Maryland. Then, on December 2, Chambers led two HUAC investigators to the place where the film was hidden and gave it to them to be developed.

A picture of Nixon and Stripling examining the microfilm Chambers provided to HUAC

The next day, Hiss announced, "During the course of examination by my counsel of Mr. Chambers in the libel action which I have brought against him in Baltimore. Mr. Chambers produced certain documents which I consider of such importance that I directed my attorneys to place them at once before the Department of Justice. This has been done, and I have offered my full cooperation to the Department of Justice and to the Grand Jury in the further investigation of this matter." For his part, Hiss would always insist that Chambers had forged the incriminating documents.

Chapter 5: The Hiss Case

A picture of the Hiss brothers arriving to speak before the grand jury

"During the first Hiss trial, Murphy and I had no direct communication. What I saw of him, I saw only in the seven days, more or less, when I was on the stand. The experience was too new to me, and I was kept too busy plucking harpoons out of my skin, to form any opinion about Murphy. In the whirling atmosphere of that courtroom, with Lloyd Paul Stryker spinning and flailing like a dervish, and Judge Kaufman snapping 'Denied' to most of the Government motions, the last thing I took much thought of was the Government's prosecutor. But his summation to the jury impressed me greatly. More important, it seems to have impressed the jury. ... The whole nation now gratefully knows that six-foot-four, stalwart figure, with the mild but firm face, and the moustache. It knows what he has done. It watched him do it. I cannot add to that knowledge, except to point out this. When Thomas Murphy decided, somewhat reluctantly, to take the Hiss Case, almost nobody had ever heard of him. Within the Justice

Department he was known as a man who had never lost a case. Otherwise, he was a man who jostled no one, for he seemed without ambition beyond his immediate work." – Whittaker Chambers

In the wake of these new revelations, the issue of whether Hiss ever knew Chambers immediately became much less important than whether he had actually spied for the Soviet Union against the United States. At the same time, the Justice Department was intent of charging Hiss for perjury. According to a United Press article, "Hiss was charged with lying when he testified that neither he nor his wife ever had turned over copies of secret State Department documents to Chambers, admitted courier for a Communist spy ring." The Associated Press reported, "Chambers asserted the typewritten sheets given him were 'pursuant to an arrangement between the defendant and his wife,' she to type them when he brought them from the State Department so that he could bring them back to the State Department in the morning. Ownership of the typewriter used in making copies and paraphrases of the documents is an important part of the government's case, Murphy continued, asserting: An F.B.I. agent asked Hiss if he had a typewriter and Hiss replied that around 1938 he had an 'office standard upright' but could not remember its brand name, though possibly it was an Underwood. … Murphy said Chambers testified that in 1937 he, Hiss and a Colonel Bykov met in New York City where they decided Hiss 'should extract documents from the State Department . . . chiefly relating to Germany and the Far East.' "

Hiss' trial began on May 31, 1949, and Thomas Murphy, the Assistant United States Attorney prosecuting the case, told the jurors, "Over a period of time in 1937 and 1938, this defendant handed over secret and confidential documents to him, Chambers, a Communist, in a wholesale fashion." Murphy assured the jury, "We will corroborate Chambers' testimony by typewriting and handwriting."

Murphy

Next, Lloyd Stryker stood to speak out for the defense, during which he told the jury he was pleased that "the days of the Klieg lights, the television, and all the paraphernalia, the propaganda which surrounded the beginning of this story [were giving way to a] quiet and fair court of justice." He told the jury Hiss had not a "blot or blemish on him," and that Chambers was the actual enemy, "a voluntary conspirator against the land that I love and you love."

Stryker and Hiss

Obviously, Chambers was the prosecution's star witness, and the United Press reported that on June 2, 1949, Chambers testified "that he was first introduced to Alger Hiss in 1934 in a Washington restaurant by Harold Ware and J Peters, alleged Communist underground leaders. Resuming his testimony on the third day of the Hiss perjury trial, Chambers, a former Communist party spy courier, said he believed Hiss at that time was employed by the Agricultural Adjustment Administration. Asked what the conversation at the meeting was, Chambers replied: 'I was to head an underground apparatus in Washington which would be separate from the previous apparatus to which Mr. Hiss had belonged." ... Chambers testified he met Hiss in June or July of 1934, and when asked to identify Hiss in the courtroom. Chambers looked toward the defendant, sitting on a bench just inside the well of the courtroom, and said softly: 'He's sitting there beside his wife. Priscilla.' Hiss and his wife remained impassive. They stared intently at Chambers."

During his cross-examination, Stryker tried again and again to impeach Chambers and impugn his character, accusing him of everything from writing a play that was "an offensive treatment of Christ" while he was in college to shacking up for a time with a prostitute named "One-Eyed Annie." While Chambers denied these charges, he freely admitted to having been "for some fourteen years an enemy and traitor of the United States of America."

After Chambers was done testifying, the prosecution next called Esther Chambers to the stand to testify about the ongoing relationship she and her husband had previously had with the Hiss family. Esther made a sympathetic witness; when asked about what school her daughter had been enrolled in some 10 years earlier, she replied, "Well, sir, I don't know about dates, and if that is...within the period in which he was in the underground. I don't know why you are trying to stump me on dates." However, Judge Stanley Kaufman would have none of it, telling her, "Now, Mrs. Chambers, no one is attempting to stump you at all. And the Court resents any such implication, and I am certain that the jury does. Nobody here is attempting to stump anybody. We are here attempting to get the facts in a case that is important for the government and very important for the defendant. And it comes with very bad grace for you to indicate that anyone is attempting to stump you....Now we don't want any more of these insinuations..."

Judge Kaufman

This response by the court gave Stryker the encouragement he needed to go after her, and the following exchange took place:

> Stryker: Now, did that not shock you as a mother [to give your young child the same alias you and Whittaker were using]? Did you not think that psychologically that was a dreadful thing to do, to take a little girl and teach her to cheat and deceive by using a false name?
> E. Chambers: Well, it did worry us.
> Stryker: Then you have some conscience?
> E. Chambers: Do I have to answer that?
>
> ...
>
> Stryker: In other words, you didn't think it was very much of a

misrepresentation to present your husband to this school as a decent citizen whereas he was--

E. Chambers: I resent that. My husband is a decent citizen, a great man.

Stryker: Was he a great, decent citizen in October, 1937?

E. Chambers: When he was in the underground?

Stryker: I just asked a simple question. Was he a great and decent citizen in October 1937. Yes or no?

E. Chambers: Yes, and always.

Stryker: And so that the jury will understand your conception: It is your idea that a man who was plotting and conspiring by any and all means to overthrow the Government of this country, who had been sneaking around for twelve years under false names, that is your conception of the great decent citizen, right?

E. Chambers: No, but if [he] then believed that is the right thing to do at the moment I believe that is a great man, who lives up to his beliefs. His beliefs may change, as they did.

Stryker: In other words, if he believed it was all right for him to sneak around the country under aliases using the means he described, you think if a man believes that kind of criminal activity is all right, you think that makes it right, is that it?

At that point, Kaufman intervened and ruled that Stryker's question was argumentative.

Next came various witnesses who testified about the events leading up to Hiss' arrest, but much of the prosecution's case hinged on whether Alger Hiss or his wife had typed the documents on the Woodstock typewriter no. 230099 that they had owned at the time. On June 16, a United Press story reported, "An FBI documents expert testified Thursday that 64 of the typed sheets in evidence in the Alger Hiss perjury trial were written with the same typewriter as that used by Hiss's wife to type letters and reports in the 1930's. ... The witness, Ramos S. Feehan, was the 30th person called to the stand by the government and the 32nd witness in the 13-day-old federal court trial. As Assistant U. S. Attorney Thomas F. Murphy began questioning Feehan, Defense Attorney Lloyd Paul Stryker arose and said the defense did not question that the handwriting on four handwritten documents in evidence was that of Hiss. The four documents are summaries of State Department secret cables which Hiss allegedly gave to Chambers. Feehan testified that he had been comparing documents since 193S and had examined 20,000 specimens in 10,000 cases. The typewriter now is in the possession of the defense."

The Hiss typewriter

It was this last detail that proved to be the surprise of the trial because the prosecution had been unable to find the typewriter in spite of an intense search. In the course of defending himself, Hiss claimed that he could not have typed the papers in question because he had already given away his typewriter to his maid, Claudia Catlett, and on June 23, the Associated Press reported, "After producing the Woodstock typewriter, defense counsel began to lay the groundwork for proving its contention that the Hisses disposed of the machine before the time of the alleged document copying. ... The defense also used the servants yesterday to bolster Hiss' denial of seeing Chambers. Mrs. Claudia Catlett, 47-year-old Negro maid for the Hisses in Washington from 1935 to 1938, testified that the typewriter in court was given to her family by Hiss in 1936 as a toy for her children. Her son, Raymond, 27, who did odd jobs for the Hisses, testified the machine remained in his family's possession until at least 1941. ... Three members of the Catlett family testified that the Woodstock typewriter on which the Baltimore papers were allegedly typed was in fact in their possession, not the Hiss's, in early 1938. Claudia Catlett thought she received the machine in mid-1936. Mike Catlett recalled that the typewriter 'was broke...the keys would jam up on you,' but on cross-examination could not remember getting the machine repaired or when the family got it from the Hiss's. Perry Catlett placed the time of the gift of the typewriter as December 1937 and recalled taking it soon thereafter to a 'repair shop at K Street just off Connecticut Avenue.'"

However, there was a problem with Perry Catlett's testimony, because according to Murphy, the shop in question did not exist until 1938. This fact seemingly undermined his testimony and that of the rest of the family.

Still, the defense was far from finished. Witnesses were brought forward to testify about Hiss' outstanding character and government service. One newspaper article noted, "Rarely has a defense team ever assembled so impressive a batch of character witnesses as appeared on behalf of Alger Hiss. The list included two U. S. Supreme Court justices, a former Solicitor General, and both former (John W. Davis) and future (Adlai Stevenson) Democratic presidential nominees. Justice Felix Frankfurter described Hiss's reputation as 'excellent.' Justice Stanley Reed said of Hiss's reputation, 'I have never heard it questioned until these matters came up.'"

Finally, the defense called Hiss himself, and according to the same article, Hiss stuck to his story: "On June 23, Alger Hiss took the stand. He admitted writing the four handwritten notes produced by Chambers, but denied any connection with the microfilm found in Chambers's pumpkin or any role in the typing of the sixty-five State Department documents. He also insisted--as he had told the grand jury in December--that he had not met Chambers on any occasion after January 1, 1937. As for the Woodstock typewriter, Hiss's 'best recollection' was that he gave it to the Catletts 'in the fall of 1937.' On cross-examination, Murphy focused on bringing out numerous inconsistencies between Hiss's trial testimony and his earlier statements."

The defense later called Priscilla Hiss to the stand. The Associated Press reported, "Questioned about various assertions by Mrs. Chambers, including testimony that the two women shared a Delaware River cottage for 10 days, Mrs. Hiss declared: 'Nothing of that kind ever happened. I have never been there. I never visited Mr. and Mrs. Chambers at any of their Baltimore homes; never drove my car 40 miles to sit in the park with Mrs. Chambers; and never sat in any park with her, with or without her baby.' Mrs. Hiss also disputed Mrs. Chambers' version of the type and arrangement of furniture in the Hiss homes in Washington." However, Priscilla's testimony was gravely impeached when Murphy showed the court a voter roll listing her as a member of the Socialist party after she denied she had ever been a Socialist.

Priscilla Hiss

In spite of this setback, Stryker still had his summation, during which he proclaimed, "This case comes down to this, 'who is telling the truth, Alger Hiss or Chambers?' and the government's burden, as I've pointed out to you so many times, is to establish beyond a reasonable doubt that it's Chambers who is telling the truth. Is there any jury in the world who could sleep with their consciences and say beyond a reasonable doubt that Chambers was the truthful man?" Stryker also attacked Chambers personally, calling him "an enemy of the Republic, a blasphemer of Christ, a disbeliever in God, with no respect for matrimony or motherhood," and a "moral leper." Stryker went on to insist that Hiss was "an honest...and falsely accused gentleman," concluding, "Ladies and gentlemen, the case will be in your hands. I beg you, I pray you to search your consciences. Alger Hiss, the long nightmare is drawing to a close. Rest well, your case, your life, your liberty are in good hands."

Next, it was Murphy's turn. Addressing the jurors, he said, "I'm very glad there is an open and long discussion about 'reasonable doubt' because the judge will tell you it's the doubt that's based upon reason. ... Who is the moral leper? Whittaker Chambers? Who is Whittaker Chambers; he is the bosom pal of his defendant. If Mr. Stryker called Mr. Chambers a moral leper, what is the defendant Hiss? What is the name of an employee of his government who takes government papers and gives them to a Communist espionage agent? What is the name of such a person? Very simple Alger Hiss was a traitor—a traitor to his country, another Benedict Arnold, another Judas Iscariot…. Hiss is a clean-cut, handsome intelligent, American-born male of some 44 years. You cannot apply reason to those facts. God gave him his looks and I assume his own diligence gave him his intelligence. Chambers is short and fat. He had bad teeth. Those are emotional factors. Mrs. Chambers is plain, severe. Mrs. Hiss is demure and attractive, and intelligent to boot—very intelligent. But those are emotional factors. Someone has said that roses that fester stink far worse than weeds, and I say that a brilliant man like this man who betrays his trust, stinks, and under that smiling face his heart is black and cancerous. He's a traitor."

As it turned out, all these statements yielded little fruit, as the jury returned after only a short debate to inform the judge that its members were "unable to agree at a verdict." Kaufman sent them back to the jury room to try again, but they remained deadlocked, so he had to declare a mistrial. Later, those who had sat behind the closed doors revealed that the vote had been 8-4 in favor of conviction, and that those with doubts believed it was possible someone else could have used Hiss' typewriter to produce the incriminating State Department documents.

Chapter 6: Waiting for the Returns to Come In

"It was the great body of the nation, which, not invariably, but in general, kept open its mind in the Hiss Case, waiting for the returns to come in. It was they who suspected what forces disastrous to the nation were at work in the Hiss Case, and had suspected that they were at work long before there was a Hiss Case…. It was they who, when the battle was over, first caught its real meaning. It was they who almost unfailingly understood the nature of the witness that I was seeking to make, as I have tested beyond question whenever I have talked to any group of them. And it was they who, in the persons of the men I have cited, produced the forces that could win a struggle whose conspicuous feature is that it was almost without leadership. From the very outset, I was in touch with that enormous force, for which I was making the effort, and from which I drew strength. … It reached me in letters and messages of encouragement and solicitude, understanding, stirring, sometimes wringing the heart. But even when they did not understand, my people were always about me. I had only to look around me to see them…" – Whittaker Chambers

Only a few months passed between the first and second Hiss trials, but enough changed around the world to help influence the ultimate outcome. For one thing, the Soviet Union tested its first atomic bomb, showing the Americans that they were now facing a serious nuclear threat from the Communist empire. Moreover, the Communist Chinese Red Army, led by Mao, drove Chiang Kai-shek to the island of Formosa (Taiwan). Finally, the United States banded with other anti-Communist countries to form the National Atlantic Treaty Organization. The result of these numerous events led to an upsurge in anti-Communist sentiment across America.

When the second trial convened on November 17, 1949, Murphy was still the prosecutor, but Stryker had been replaced by Claude Cross and Judge Kaufman was replaced by Judge Henry W. Goddard.

Cross and Hiss

Judge Goddard

Julian Wadleigh, who had testified briefly during the first trial, was called again to the stand this time around, and according to an Associated Press story on November 18, "Counsel for Alger Hiss sprung a new line of defense today, contending that secret government papers obtained by Whittaker Chambers came from Julian Wadleigh, former State Department employee. ... Hiss' defense counsel told a jury of eight women and four men that the documents on which the government built its case against Hiss in the first trial actually came from the hands of Wadleigh 'The microfilms which will be entered into evidence are not photographs of originals which went to (Francis B.) Sayre's office (in the State Department) Cross said. Hiss worked under Sayre, then Assistant Secretary of State. 'They are carbons which went to the trade agreement office where Julian Wadleigh was. The microfilm came from Julian Wadleigh.'"

Wadleigh

Unfortunately for Hiss, there were problems with this claim, specifically the fact that Wadleigh would have also had to obtain Hiss' own handwritten notes. Also, it was difficult to believe that Wadleigh could have both stolen the documents and returned them without getting caught.

In an even more aggressive attempt to discredit Chambers, Cross introduced Dr. Carl A. Binger as an expert witness. A psychiatrist, Binger had studied Chambers' writings and his demeanor at the trial. Based on this information, Binger testified, "I think Mr. Chambers is suffering from a condition known as psychopathic personality, which is a disorder of character, of which the outstanding features are behavior of what we call an amoral or an asocial and delinquent nature. I mean that amoral behavior is behavior that does not take account the ordinary accepted conventions of morality; and asocial behavior is behavior which has not regard for the good of society and of individuals, and is therefore frequently destructive of both. [The symptoms] include chronic, persistent and repetitive lying; they include stealing; they include acts of deception and misrepresentations; they include alcoholism and drug addiction; abnormal sexuality; vagabondage; panhandling; inability to form stable attachments; and a tendency to make false accusations. May I say that in addition to what is commonly recognized by the layman as lying, there is a peculiar kind of lying known as pathological lying, and a peculiar kind of tendency to make false accusations known as pathological accusations, which are frequently found in the psychopathic personality."

Even in an era where Freud's work was still popular, it was not difficult for Murphy to dismantle Binger's testimony and even his credibility. One observer later noted, "Mr. Murphy just wanted plain answers to plain questions--about the most alarming assignment anyone would wish on a psychiatrist." Again and again, Murphy hammered away at Binger's assumptions that Chambers was a psychopath merely because he had lied on his passport, left college after only a few days, and had hid the microfilm in a pumpkin. Mentioning that Binger had noted that Chambers frequently looked up at the ceiling while testifying, Murphy observed that his own assistant had observed Binger looking up more than 50 times during his own testimony. In reference to Binger's claim that "untidiness" in dress was a symptom of psychopathic personality, Murphy rhetorically asked him what the public should make of other untidy people such as Albert Einstein or Thomas Edison.

Perhaps the most humorous exchange concerned the doctor's evaluation of the pumpkin as a proper hiding place for the microfilm.

> MURPHY: You say that a man who was living on a farm in 1948, who puts pretty valuable papers in a pumpkin that he has hollowed out right by his door, is bizarre?

> BINGER: I say the act is bizarre.

> MURPHY: The act is bizarre?

> BINGER: Because it is unusual. Perhaps there is one other example in history that you have given.

> MURPHY: If, Doctor, you assume that these microfilms were previously in his house and he moved them from room to room, and that the day that he put them in the pumpkin was the day that he was going to leave his farm, and assume further that there were different people in and about the farm looking for things, wouldn't you say, Doctor, that that was a pretty good hiding place?

> BINGER: It was.

> MURPHY: No matter how bizarre it was?

> BINGER: It certainly was a good hiding place, yes.

> …

> MURPHY: Well, how about the mother of Moses hiding the little child in the

bulrushes? Was that bizarre?

BINGER: Well, she could hardly put it in a safe deposit vault.

MURPHY: Now, Doctor, you don't tell us that all things that don't fit in safe deposit boxes are therefore bizarre, do you?

BINGER: No, I don't.

MURPHY: I am asking you, Doctor, whether the action of Moses' mother in putting the young child in the bulrushes was bizarre behavior?

BINGER: I don't know the circumstances and I wouldn't know where else she had to hide the child. If that was the only place, it certainly was not bizarre.

If the defense team thought their witnesses would help prove Hiss's innocence, Murphy had one he believed would further the government's case against him. During the second trial Judge Goddard allowed a new witness, whom his predecessor had barred, to testify: Hede Massing, who had once been a spy for the Soviet Union. The Associated Press reported on December 10, "Appearing as a government witness yesterday in Hiss' second perjury trial, Mrs. Hede Massing, one-time Viennese actress, pictured herself and Hiss as friendly rivals in the underground. … Mrs. Massing said she met Hiss in 1935 when she was 'working for the Communist party.' The meeting, she said was at the home of Noel Field, who, like Hiss, was then an official in the U. S. State Department. Mrs. Massing said she and Hiss argued over which of them would get the services of Field in their separate underground cells."

Massing

The second trial ended up being three weeks longer than the first as each side tried their hardest to sway the jury in their favor. Admitting during his summation that the documents Chambers provided were indeed typed on the Woodstock typewriter, Cross nonetheless insisted that "it is not the question of what typewriter was used, but who the typist was." He then went on to hypothesize that Chambers himself, or perhaps another communist, had gotten possession of Hiss' typewriter after he got rid of it and typed the pages themselves in order to frame Hiss. This hypothesis was obviously thin, given that it would require the juror to believe that someone knew where the typewriter was and to whom it had belonged, after which someone would have to be able to steal it, use it, and return it without its absence being detected.

Murphy, on the other hand, claimed to have "immutable" evidence of the conspiracy between Chambers and Hiss. He insisted that Hiss was indeed a traitor "in love with their philosophy, not ours."

Ultimately, Murphy successfully convinced the jurors. On January 20, 1950, they returned a verdict: "We find the defendant guilty on the first count and guilty on the second." Goddard thanked them for what he called a "just verdict" before retiring to his chambers to contemplate Hiss' sentence. Five days later, he returned to the courtroom and asked Hiss if he had anything to say before he handed down the sentence. After thanking the judge, Hiss declared "that in the future the full facts of how Whittaker Chambers was able to carry out forgery by typewriter will be disclosed." Goddard then imposed the maximum sentence of 5 years on the convicted perjurer.

A picture of Hiss in handcuffs after being convicted

A picture of Hiss on the way to jail

Less than two weeks after Hiss was convicted, an obscure Republican Senator from Wisconsin spoke to the Republican Women's Club of Wheeling, West Virginia to commemorate Lincoln Day. In his speech, he claimed, "The reason why we find ourselves in a position of impotency is not because our only powerful potential enemy has sent men to invade our shores, but rather because of the traitorous actions of those who have been treated so well by this Nation. It has not been the less fortunate or members of minority groups who have been selling this Nation out, bulk rather those who have had all the benefits that the wealthiest nation on earth has had to offer--the finest homes, the finest college education, and the finest jobs in Government we can give. This is glaringly true in the State Department. There the bright young men who are born with silver spoons in their mouths are the ones who have been worst. ... This, ladies and gentlemen, gives you somewhat of a picture of the type of individuals who have been helping to shape our foreign policy. In my opinion the State Department, which is one of the most important government departments, is thoroughly infested with Communists. I have in my hand 57 cases of Individuals who would appear to be either card carrying members or certainly loyal to the Communist Party, but who nevertheless are still helping to shape our foreign policy. … This brings us down to the case of one Alger Hiss who is important not as an individual any more, but rather because he is so representative of a group in the State Department. It is unnecessary to go over the sordid events showing how he sold out the Nation which had given him so much. Those are rather fresh in all of our minds."

The Senator's name was Joseph McCarthy, and America's hunt for communists was about to turn into a hysteria.

McCarthy

Hiss quickly appealed his conviction, but on December 7, 1950, the Second Circuit Court of Appeals denied his appeal and affirmed his conviction, concluding, "The charge of the court was clear and comprehensive with such due attention to detail in respect to the law relevant to the facts which might be found upon the evidence that all the requests to charge which should have been granted were adequately covered. We find no error in it. The effort to have the judgment arrested and the indictment dismissed was induced by a clearly untenable theory that the statute of limitations had barred the prosecution of the offense charged in the indictment."

Hiss then appealed to the Supreme Court of the United States, but the high court refused to hear the case. Part of the reason centered on Hiss' past; due to his time spent under Justice Holmes, a majority of the justices felt compelled to recuse themselves based on being connected to either Hiss or his case or both.

Thus, with his appeals exhausted, Hiss began serving his sentence in the Lewisburg Federal Penitentiary in Pennsylvania. He was released 44 months later, having been a model prisoner who earned an early release for good behavior. He spent the rest of his life denying that he had ever spied for anyone.

Meanwhile, Whittaker Chambers published his own account of the trial and the events surrounding it in an autobiography called *Witness*. When it came out in 1952, the *New York Times* review noted, "It throws more light on the conspiratorial and religious character of modern Communism, on the tangled complex of motives which led men and women of goodwill to immolate themselves on the altar of a fancied historical necessity, than all of the hundred great books of the past combined." An actor in California named Ronald Reagan read the book and later claimed it led him to abandon the Democratic Party and become a Republican. He maintained the book was "the counterrevolution of the intellectuals" and showed "a generation's disenchantment with statism and its return to eternal truths and fundamental values."

1952 also saw Richard Nixon, who had risen to prominence for helping nail Hiss, elected as Vice President of the United States under Eisenhower. The Republican Party began shaping itself as tough on communism, and Barry Goldwater continued this tradition, as did Reagan, who saw the "Evil Empire" collapse just a few years after he left office.

With the collapse of the Soviet Union and the end of the Cold War, long-held secrets came to light, and one of the biggest secrets was the fact that the United States Army Signal Intelligence Service, which became the National Security Agency, had broken the codes used by the Soviet Union's intelligence services in the 1940s. Under the code name Venona, the program decrypted thousands of coded messages that revealed the extensive contacts between the Soviet Union and the Communist Party USA, contacts that clearly showed the latter to be directly controlled by Moscow. They also showed the extensive spy networks built in the 1930s and 1940s, and it proved that Soviet-directed Communists had indeed infiltrated the federal government. However, these men and women were only identified by code names

Such was the sensitive nature of Venona that knowledge of its existence was carefully limited. Only the NSA and the FBI were aware of the secret, and even in the FBI the real source of information from the decrypts was limited to a handful of people, including J. Edgar Hoover. The NSA would give information from the decrypts to the FBI, whose agents would then conduct investigations to uncover the true identities of the men and women who were working for the Soviets.

One decrypt, #1822, describes an agent codenamed ALES who headed a spy ring referred to as the "neighbors." The decrypt was dated March 30, 1945 and was sent from the Soviet Embassy in Washington to Moscow. It mentioned that ALES had been at the Yalta conference and then traveled to Moscow. Extensive analyses by the NSA, the FBI, and historians have all concluded that there is likely only one person who fits the identity of ALES: Alger Hiss.

Chapter 7: Opened Files

The Rosenbergs

"The FBI opened files on both Rosenbergs in the late 1930s, when the nation was still wrestling with poverty and when the fear of war focused on Nazi Germany. Both the Rosenbergs, according to FBI informants, were unionists, affiliated with the American Labor Party, supporters of the Loyalist government in Spain which was defending itself against a Nazi-financed rebellion led by General Francisco Franco. ... The Rosenbergs were also reported by FBI informants to have been present at left-wing public rallies, and were said to have regularly read the Communist newspaper, the Daily Worker and other radical literature. Although Julius gradually evolved into a Communist or near-Communist, he seems to have been intellectually attracted to Communism rather than driven to it by his experiences. He does not appear to have felt especially deprived by poverty, probably because he had a nourishing, affectionate life within his family and, at a fairly early age, with Ethel. He had a practical turn of mind, and his radical leanings didn't leave him with a distaste for business. He also had an orderly sense, to which his preference for socialism over capitalism may have been related; as a young man in the Depression years, he saw capitalism as chaotic and anarchistic, driven by uncontrollable individualistic forces, while socialism appeared to hold out the promise of a rationally planned economic order." – Emily Alman, *Exoneration*

They were both born in New York, the city that never sleeps. Their families were Jewish and their parents had come to the United States as part of the wave of Jewish immigrants that fled Europe at that the turn of the previous century. She was born first, on September 25, 1915 and dreamed of being an actress. He was born later, on May 12, 1918, and grew up on the Lower East Side. They both attended Seward High School, where she graduated at the young age of 15. She worked as a secretary, while he completed high school and attended City College of New York. They met in 1936 at a young people's event, and three years later, when he graduated with a degree in electrical engineering, they got married.

It might have been a classic American tale but for the fact that Ethel Greenglass and Julius Rosenberg first met at a meeting of the Young Communist League USA. Such political affiliations were obviously not part of the mainstream, but while they were dating and during the early years of their marriage, the young Rosenbergs did what others their ages were doing. Julius got a job and joined a union, albeit the rather radical Federation of Architects, Engineers, Chemists, and Technicians (FAECT). There he made friends, some of whom would later become infamous, including Morton Sobell, Joel Barr, and William Perl.

Sobell (on the left) in East Germany in the 1970s

Joel Barr

William Perl

Just before the United States joined World War II, Julius joined the U.S. Army Signal Corps, where he did a good enough job that he was made an inspector in 1942, allowing the young couple to move into a spacious three bedroom apartment. But by this time, the couple was also deeply involved in the American Communist Party, with Julius serving as a chairman in the Industrial Division while Ethel worked behind the scenes and raised their two sons, Michael and Robert.

A few years later, in 1945, the Army learned about Julius' involvement with Communism and fired him from his Signal Corps job. The timing was somewhat ironic because in 1943, Julius and Ethel had suddenly left the Communist Party, giving the impression that they had perhaps seen the error of their political ways.

As it turned out, it appears almost the exact opposite was true. According to Max Elitcher, Julius approached him in 1944 about selling information to the Soviets. He would later testify, "He called me and reminded me of our school friendship and came to my home. After a while, he asked if my wife would leave the room, that he wanted to talk to me in private. She did. Then he began talking about the job that the Soviet Union was doing in the war effort and how at present a good deal of military information was being denied them by some interests in the United States, and because of that their effort was being impeded. He said there were many people who were implementing aid to the Soviet Union by providing classified information about military equipment, and so forth, and asked whether in my capacity at the Bureau of Ordnance working on anti-aircraft devices, and computer control of firing missiles, would I turn information over to him? He told me that any information I gave him would be taken to New York, processed photographically and would be returned overnight--so it would not be missed. The process would be safe as far as I am concerned."

Elitcher

Turning American intelligence over to the Soviets would sound much worse in 1950, but at the time the Russians were America's allies against the Nazis in the middle of a war that still had an uncertain conclusion. It's only natural that Communist sympathizers believed it was not just unfair but unwise to deny the Soviets information they could use to defend themselves against the German invasion.

Meanwhile, both the United States and Germany were both working on a weapon destined to change the course of history. America's very secret Manhattan Project was in the midst of developing an atomic bomb, the most sought after weapon on earth, and no one wanted it more than the USSR. Thus, Julius was ecstatic when he learned, in July 1944, that David Greenglass, Ethel's brother, was going to be working as a machinist on the Manhattan Project.

A few months later, in November, Julius persuaded his brother-in-law to provide him with information he gathered while on the job. Greenglass later described one of their intimate meetings: "He came up to the apartment and he got me out of bed and we went into another room so my wife could dress. He said to me that he wanted to know what I had for him. I told him 'I think I have a pretty good description of the atom bomb.'" Rosenberg gave Greenglass $200 and said he would return later for the description.

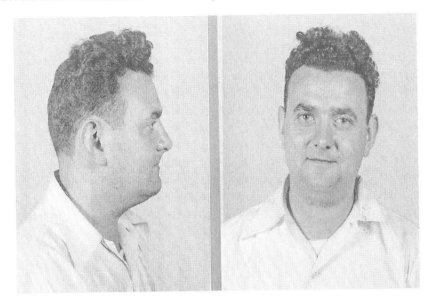

David Greenglass

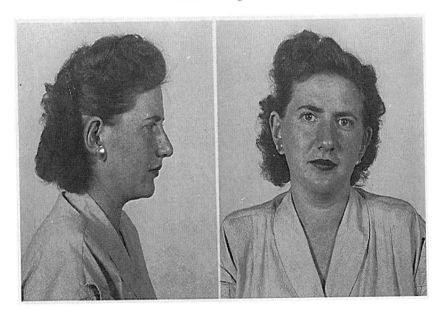

Ruth Greenglass

Greenglass also testified that on another occasion, "[Julius] told me that if he wanted to get in touch with the Russians, he had a means of communicating with them in a motion picture theater, an alcove where he would put microfilm or messages and the Russians would pick it up. If he wanted to see them in person, he would put a message in there and by prearrangement they would meet in some lonely spot in Long Island."

In December 1944, Julius Rosenberg passed along to the Soviets a proximity fuse he had obtained from Greenglass, and a month later, Greenglass passed on information about a high-explosive lens that was being used in the bomb. In the latter case, however, Greenglass did not hand it to Rosenberg directly but to Harry Gold, a chemist and courier for several Soviet spy rings. Greenglass said of his first meeting with Gold, "There was a knock on the door and I opened it. We had just completed eating breakfast, and there was a man standing in the hallway who asked if I was Mr. Greenglass and I said, yes. He stepped through the door and said, 'Julius sent me,' and I said, 'Oh' and walked to my wife's purse, took out the wallet and took out the matched part of the Jell-O box. He produced his piece and we checked them and they fitted, and the identification was made. I offered him something to eat and he said he had already eaten. He just wanted to know if I had any information, and I said, 'I have some but I will have to write it up. If you come back in the afternoon, I will give it to you.' I started to tell him about one of the people who would be good material for recruiting into espionage work-- He cut me short and he left and I got to work on the report."

Now on the course of betrayal, Greenglass moved quickly: "I got out some 8 by 10 ruled white paper, and I drew some sketches of a lens mold and how they are set up in the experiment, and I gave a description of the experiment. ...I also gave him a list of possible recruits for espionage. ...at 2:30-- I gave him my report in an envelope and he gave me an envelope, which I felt and realized there was money in it and I put it in my pocket. ... Gold said, 'Will it be enough?' and I said, 'Well, it will be plenty for the present.' And he said 'You need it' and we went into a side discussion about the fact that my wife had a miscarriage earlier in the spring, and he said, 'Well, I will see what I can do about getting some more money for you.' My wife and I counted it later. There was $500-- I gave it to her."

Gold

When Soviet leader Joseph Stalin was first informed by the other leaders of the Allies about the existence of a new secret weapon known as the atomic bomb, he had to feign surprise and ignorance about it. In fact, Stalin's regime had been working on a nuclear weapons program since 1942, relying greatly upon successful Soviet espionage to help lead the way. With intelligence sources connected to the Manhattan Project, Stalin was able to keep abreast of the Allies' progress toward creating an atomic bomb, and by 1945, the Soviets already had a working blueprint of America's first atomic bombs. On August 29, 1949, the Soviets successfully tested an atomic bomb, and with that, the Soviet Union became the second nation after the U.S. to develop and possess nuclear weapons.

Chapter 8: A Practiced Hand

"Irving Saypol was a practiced hand at converting courtroom trials into theater. Some months before being assigned to the Rosenberg-Sobell case he had persuaded a jury, without citing a single act of violence, that books on history and philosophy could be truly incendiary, which resulted in prison sentences for ten Communist leaders. … Unlike many other cities in which the electorate had moved to the political right as a result of the Cold War, New York City voters favored New Deal and liberal candidates for public office and, in the immediate post-war years, had elected two Communists to the City Council. … Candidate-jurors were also drawn from at least a dozen small towns north of the city when…there were 'not enough' candidate-jurors among New York City's nearly 8,000,000 residents. As a result, jury panels could be drawn that had only a passing resemblance to the overall demographics of the city. Five of the jurors at the Rosenberg-Sobell trial were not from New York City at all, but from White Plains, Mamaroneck, Scarsdale, Dobbs Ferry, and Mt. Vernon. A second step in diluting the New York City 'mix' was Judge Kaufman's decision to pass the jury candidates through a political 'filter' test…which would eliminate any candidates who admitted to reading newspapers or journals, or having been members of organizations that had been declared subversive by the U.S. Attorney General." – Emily Alman, *Exoneration*

One of the people working on the bomb in Los Alamos during the war was Klaus Fuchs, a British physicist. He met with a Soviet agent known only as Raymond on two separate occasions in 1945, providing him with design notes on the bomb both times. He would be arrested in February 1950, and upon seeing the damning evidence presented before him, Fuchs decided to confess in hopes of getting a lighter sentence. He also shared information with the authorities about the spy known only as Raymond.

Fuchs

The FBI eventually determined that Raymond was actually Harry Gold. Gold also subsequently confessed, and he said of his first meeting with Fuchs, "He obviously worked with our people before and he is fully aware of what he is doing... He is a mathematical physicist... most likely a very brilliant man to have such a position at his age (he looks about 30). We took a long walk after dinner...He is a member of a British mission to the U.S. working under the direct control of the U.S. Army...He says there is much being withheld from the British. Even Niels Bohr, who is now in the country incognito as Nicholas Baker, has not been told everything."

Based on the information they had gathered, the authorities next questioned David Greenglass about the implosion lens that was a critical part of the bomb. Greenglass not only confessed to passing information to Gold but also implicated his own wife, Ruth, as well as his sister Ethel and his brother-in-law Julius.

FBI agents arrived at the Rosenbergs' apartment a little after 8:00 a.m. on the morning of June

16, 1950 and asked Julius to go with them to answer a few questions. Having had tremendous success getting the others they had questioned to confess, they assumed Rosenberg would also crack quickly under the pressure but they were wrong. Instead, Julius adamantly maintained his innocence and immediately hired a lawyer, Emanuel Bloch, to represent him.

A little more than a month passed as the FBI continued to gather information from both David Greenglass and his wife, Ruth, but finally, on July 17, 1950, the agents returned to the Rosenbergs' apartment and arrested Julius. They also swarmed the apartment and took it apart piece by piece, looking for more evidence.

Bloch

A picture of Julius being booked

At this time, the FBI did not intend to arrest Ethel, as they had very little evidence against her, but the agency hoped that by threatening her, it would be enough to leverage testimony out of Julius. J. Edgar Hoover himself insisted, "There is no question that if Julius Rosenberg would furnish details of his extensive espionage activities it would be possible to proceed against other individuals. Proceeding against his wife might serve as a lever in these matters." To that end, the FBI arrested Ethel on August 11.

Hoover

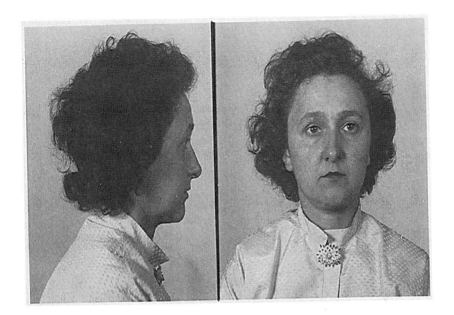

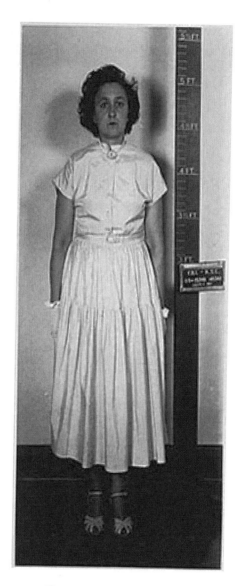

Pictures of Ethel being booked

Around this time, the entire spy ring began to unravel. Joel Barr, an old friend of Julius's, fled the country for France. Morton Sobell also left, taking his family with him to Mexico City, and Alfred Sarant made a similar journey. Meanwhile, William Perl, another scientist, testified before the grand jury that he had never met Julius, only to be charged a little while later with perjury.

Max Elitcher, a friend of both Sobell and Julius, attempted to save himself by cooperating with the investigators and implicating the two men. He would testify about how he came across some valuable information in 1948: "Sobell said he had some valuable information in the house, something he should have given to Julius Rosenberg some time ago. It was too valuable to be destroyed and too dangerous to keep around. He said he wanted to deliver it to Rosenberg that night. He said he was tired and he wanted me to go along. He might not be able to make the trip back. He took a 33 millimeter film can. We drove to Catherine Slip. I parked the car facing the East River. He left with the can. I waited. He came back about a half hour later and as we drove off, I said, 'Well, what does Julie think about my being followed?' He said, 'Don't be concerned about it; it is ok.'" With this story in hand, the FBI managed to get Sobell back from Mexico and charge him with espionage.

United States v Julius Rosenberg, Ethel Rosenberg, and Morton Sobell convened under dreary New York spring skies on March 6, 1951. Each of the three being tried was accused of conspiracy to commit espionage, a capital crime that carried a death sentence upon conviction. The prosecutor, Irving Saypol, and the judge, Irving Kaufman, had just recently worked on the case of alleged Soviet spy Alger Hiss, who was ultimately convicted of perjury after a lengthy saga that remains nearly as controversial as the case against the Rosenbergs.

Saypol

Kaufman

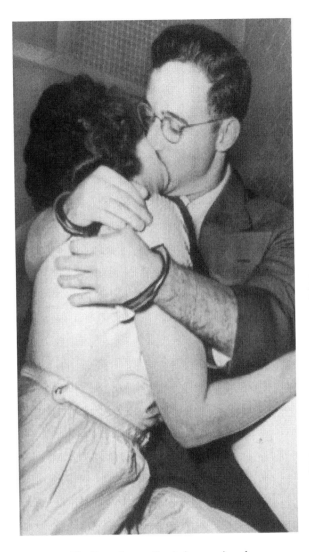

The Rosenbergs after being arraigned

In concluding his opening statement, Saypol insisted that by passing information about "the weapons the Soviet Union could use to destroy us," the defendants "have committed the most serious crime which can be committed against the people of this country." Trying to counter the prosecution's patriotic appeal, Bloch asked for a "fair shake in the American way. We ask you to keep your minds open. We ask you to judge these defendants, American citizens, as you would want to be judged yourself if you were sitting as a defendant."

The prosecution then called Max Elitcher to the stand and focused on his interaction with

Sobell. In his cross-examination, Bloch attempted to impeach Elitcher in such a way as to make his testimony less believable, asking him, "Did you ever sign a loyalty oath for the Federal Government?" When he admitted he had, the following exchange took place:

E. H. BLOCH: Do you know the contents of the oath you signed and swore to?

ELITCHER: I signed a statement saying that I was not or had not been a member of an organization that was dedicated to overthrow the Government by force and violence. I don't remember whether the statement specifically mentioned the Communist Party or not.

E.H. BLOCH: At the time you verified that oath, did you believe you were lying when you concealed your membership in the Communist Party?

ELITCHER: Yes. I did.

E. H. BLOCH: So you have lied under oath?

ELITCHER: Yes.

E. H. BLOCH: Were you worried about it?

ELITCHER: Yes...

E. H. BLOCH: AS a matter of fact, didn't you leave the Government service to try to get a job in private industry because you were afraid you might be prosecuted for perjury?

ELITCHER: That is not the entire reason for my leaving.

E. R. BLOCH: But that was one of the substantial reasons?

ELITCHER: I would say, yes.

Bloch also introduced the jury to the idea that Elitcher was only testifying to save himself, not out of any sense of wanting to right a wrong:

E. R.BLOCH: Now when you were interrogated by the FBI for the first time, did that fear of prosecution persist in your mind?

ELITCHER: Yes, I realized what the implications might be.

E. H. BLOCH: You felt that the Government had something over you, didn't you?

ELITCHER: I couldn't tell; I thought, yes, perhaps. ... I didn't know what information the FBI had; I had no idea. However, I felt that I didn't want to fight the case. When they came to me, I freely told them the story, and as they might know about it anyway, I felt the only course was to tell the complete story, which I did.

E. H. BLOCH: It wasn't out of any sense of patriotism that you told the FBI the story?

ELITCHER: Well, in a sense, yes.

E. H. BLOCH: It was to save your own skin, wasn't it?

ELITCHER: No, because I didn't know what would happen to my skin even when I told the story--and I knew of nothing I was doing that would save my skin....
From the first time that I was approached by the FBI, I decided I would tell the whole complete story. I had no idea at the time of what would happen to me. Frankly, I didn't know whether I would be arrested the same day, and to this day, I don't know what is going to happen, and I decided that purely on the basis that I would tell the whole truth and at least in the future I would not be subjected to any perjury, and I would hope in that way I would come out in the best way. I could see no other course but to tell the truth."

After a while, Bloch yielded to Edward Kuntz, who was representing Morton Sobell. He raised an issue concerning Elitcher's visits to a psychiatrist, which carried a substantial stigma in America at the time. In response, Saypol insisted that Elitcher be allowed time to explain to the court why he had gone to such visits, but this may not have helped. Elitcher told the court, "Well, after our marriage we found that we had domestic difficulties and we found it difficult to live with each other. We found that I had personality problems and she had personality problems which prevented a happy existence together. I found it difficult to meet with people to have a good time, to talk in front of an audience. I think, to jump a step, without the aid that I went to, it would be difficult for me to present myself in front of this audience in this matter, and because of that my wife decided that she would attempt to correct her problems which were of a similar nature to mine, but perhaps not exactly the same. She went to a psychiatrist and felt that she was being benefited by it, but because I wasn't going, so that it would be a two-way arrangement, that both of us would be improved by it, she insisted that I go. It was upon her insistence that I finally did go to a psychiatrist. It was only after I had gone and had been able to recognize some of my problems, that our married life did adjust itself, and I will say right now that it couldn't be much happier as married life goes."

Next, the prosecution called David Greenglass to the stand. Saypol's assistant, Roy Cohn, questioned him about a number of issues and then came to the matter of the sketch he had made the previous year for Rosenberg. Bloch objected to a copy of the sketch being introduced to the jury since it had been drawn from memory, but Kaufman allowed the sketch to be admitted, saying, "The weight to be given it will be . . . entirely up to the jury. It is being done for the purpose of permitting the jury to visualize what was turned over, and only insofar as that. It is not being introduced as the document which was given to Gold, because for apparent reasons the Government couldn't introduce that at this time..."

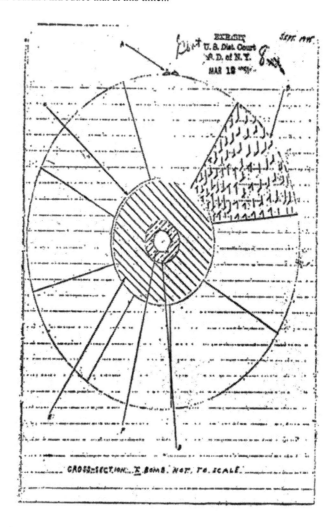

Greenglass' sketch of an implosion-type nuclear weapon design that he gave Julius Rosenberg to pass along to the Soviets

During the cross examination, Bloch again attempted to portray the witness as someone who could not be trusted:

E. H. BLOCH You knew at that time, did you not, that you were engaging in the commission of a very serious crime?

GREENGLASS: I did. . .

E. H. BLOCH: Did it occur to you at the time that you finally said to your wife, 'I will do this' and then transmitted to her certain information that there was a possible penalty of death for espionage?

GREENGLASS: Yes.

E. H. BLOCH: Are you aware that you are smiling?

GREENGLASS: Not very. . . .

E. H. BLOCH: And from the time in the latter part of November 1944, during your entire career in the Army, you continued to spy, did you not?

GREENGLASS: I did.

E. H. BLOCH: And you received money for that, did you not?

GREENGLASS: I did.

E. H. BLOCH: You received $500 from Harry Gold in Albuquerque, New Mexico for that, did you not?

GREENGLASS: I did.

E. H. BLOCH: Did you ever offer to return that money?

GREENGLASS: I did not.

Bloch also implicitly challenged Greenglass' sanity by asking the witness, "After you were arraigned, were you taken to jail and put in solitary confinement?" Greenglass replied, "Yes, for three days. The reason I was confined, was because there was an erroneous story in the newspapers that I was going to commit suicide; so the keeper felt, well, he wasn't going to take it on himself, so he had me put in solitary and had my laces taken off my shoes and my belt taken away from me so I wouldn't commit suicide. That was the whole story. There was no other reason."

In trying to turn the jury against Greenglass, Bloch dug deep, asking, "When you went to high school and Brooklyn Polytech, did you fail in your subjects?" Greenglass admitted, "I was quite young at the time, about eighteen, and I liked to play around more than I liked to go to school, so

I cut classes almost the whole term. Simple. I failed them all." Bloch also questioned the Greenglass' military record, compelling the witness to concede, "I did my work as a soldier and produced what I had to produce, and there was no argument about my work, and since the information went to a supposed ally at the time, I had no qualms or doubts that I deserved the honorable discharge. ... In the light of today's events, I was not entitled to an honorable discharge."

At one point, Greenglass described a strange sort of relationship with Julius Rosenberg: "I had a kind of hero worship there and I did not want my hero to fail, and that I was doing the wrong thing by him. That is exactly why I did not stop the thing after I had the doubts. ... I had plenty of headaches and I felt the thousand dollars was not coming out of Julius Rosenberg's pocket. It was coming out of the Russians' pocket and it didn't bother me one bit to take it, or the $4,000 either." Bloch later challenged this by asking, "Do you remember an incident in the corner candy story at Houston and Avenue D when your brother, Bernie, had to separate both of you?" Again, Greenglass seemed to win the jury over with his honesty and humility when he said, "It slipped my mind. I don't recall if I actually hit him. It was some violent quarrel over something in the business. I don't recall exactly what it was. As a matter of fact, I didn't even recall the fight until just this moment. ... We were very friendly after that."

One of the critical things the government sought to prove at trial was that the Rosenbergs gave the Soviet Union information that was actually vital to their weapons programs. To shore up this impression for the jury, Saypol at one point temporarily interrupted Greenglass' testimony and called Walter Koski to the stand. A physicist with the Atomic Energy Commission, Koski carefully explained to the jury the importance of the lens mold that Greenglass passed on to the Soviets. When asked if the Soviets might have been able to get information on it anywhere else, Koski testified, "To the best of my knowledge and all of my colleagues who were involved in this field, there was no information in textbooks or technical journals on this particular subject." Saypol then asked, "And up to that point and continuing right up until this trial, has the information relating to the lens mold and the lens and the experimentation to which you have testified continued to be secret information?" Koski replied, "It still is."

Saypol then addressed Kaufman, asking, "Will your Honor allow a statement for the record in that respect? The Atomic Energy Committee has declassified this information under the Atomic Energy Act and has made the ruling as authorized by Congress that subsequent to the trial it is to be reclassified."

With this allowed, he took up the issue again:

> SAYPOL: Can you tell us, Doctor, whether a scientific expert in the field you were engaged in could glean enough information from the exhibits in evidence so as to learn the nature of the object of the experiment that was involved in the sketches in evidence?

KOSKI: From these sketches and from Mr. Greenglass' descriptions, this gives one sufficient information, one who is familiar with the field, to indicate what the principle and the idea is here.

Saypol: Would I be exaggerating if I were to say colloquially that one expert, interested in finding out what was going on at Los Alamos, could get enough from those exhibits in evidence which you have before you to reveal what was going on at Los Alamos?

Koski: One could.

Chapter 9: According to Ruth Greenglass

"The Greenglasses believed that they had been under surveillance for months before David Greenglass' arrest in mid-June 1950, and became certain of it in May, when the surveillance appears to have been deliberately made obvious to them, serving as an additional intensification of the state of apprehension in which they lived. According to Ruth Greenglass, as reported by Robert H. Goldman, an attorney with the O. John Rogge law firm representing the Greenglasses, they had been under surveillance by the FBI for several weeks. In particular, they had noticed a car of the Acme Construction Company, 1400 First Avenue in Manhattan. She ascertained there was no such Company. Although Greenglass' first statement to the FBI when he was arrested in June 1950, was never made available, he appears to have acknowledged the existence of an espionage operation. ...he elaborated on it by naming his wife as having had a hand in recruiting him at the behest of Julius Rosenberg. ... There is no indication Ruth Greenglass felt astonished or betrayed when she learned David had implicated her in the conspiracy. She quickly made it clear to the prosecutors the cooperation of her husband depended on her not being indicted." – Emily Alman, *Exoneration*

One of the things that seemed to catch the public's attention during the trial was the testimony of the wives involved. In 1950s America, the idea that an otherwise normal American housewife could be spying for the Russians both horrified and fascinated many.

When she was called to the stand, Ruth Greenglass told the jury how her own brother-in-law Julius had asked her to approach her husband: "I told my husband that I knew that he was working on the atomic bomb. He asked me how I knew and who had told me. I said that I had been to Julius Rosenberg's house and that he had told me that David's work was on the atomic bomb, and he asked me how Julius knew it and I told him of the conversation we had had, that Julius had said they spent two years getting in touch with people who would enable him to do work directly for the Russian people, that his friends, the Russians, had told him that the work was on the atomic bomb, that the bomb had dangerous radiation effects, that it was a very destructive weapon and that the scientific basis, the information on the bomb should be made available to Soviet Russia..."

James Kilsheimer, a member of the prosecution team, then asked Ruth to recall her original conversation with the Rosenbergs. She testified, "Julius said that I might have noticed that for some time he and Ethel had not been actively pursuing any Communist Party activities, that they didn't buy the Daily Worker at the usual newsstand; that for two years he had been trying to get in touch with people who would assist him to be able to help the Russian people more directly other than just his membership in the Communist Party, and he went on to tell me that he knew that David was working on the atomic bomb and I asked him how he knew, because I had received an affidavit from the War Department telling me--I said that I had received an affidavit from the War Department telling me that my mail to David would be censored and his to me, because he was working on a top secret project. And he said--I wanted to know how he knew what David was doing. He said that his friends had told him that David was working on the atomic bomb, and he went on to tell me that the atomic bomb was the most destructive weapon used so far, that it had dangerous radiation effects that the United States and Britain were working on this project jointly and that he felt that the information should be shared with Russia, who was our ally at the time, because if all nations had the information then one nation couldn't use the bomb as a threat against another. He said that he wanted me to tell my husband, David, that he should give information to Julius to be passed on to the Russians."

Next, Kilsheimer asked, "And what information did he ask you to obtain from your husband if he should be willing to do it?" Ruth replied, "He wanted a physical description of the project at Los Alamos, the approximate number of people employed, the names of some of the scientists who were working there--something about whether the place was camouflaged, what the security measures were and the relative distance of the project to Albuquerque and Santa Fe. ... My husband did not give me an immediate answer; at first he, too, refused, and the following day he told me that he would consent to do this. ... He said that Los Alamos had formerly been a riding academy, that it was forty miles from Santa Fe and about 110 miles from Albuquerque, that the project itself was on the top of a hill and it was secluded; you could hardly see it until you were almost on top of it; that there was a guard at the entrance at all times, and everyone was checked going in and out. He told me the names of the scientists, Dr. Urey, Dr. Oppenheimer, Kistiakowsky, Niels Bohr. David told me that he worked in an experimental shop, that he made models from blueprints that scientists brought in to him. ... I told him to be very careful in getting the information, not to take any papers, not to take any blueprints, not to be obvious in seeking information from other people, and be careful not to get involved in political discussions."

Kilsheimer then asked Ruth about her conversation with Ethel Rosenberg at this time. She continued, "Well, Ethel said that she was tired, and I asked her what she had been doing. She said she had been typing; and I asked her if she had found David's notes hard to distinguish. She said no, she was used to his handwriting. Then she said that Julie, too, was tired; that he was very busy; he ran around a good deal; that all his time and his energies were used in this thing; that was the most important thing to him; that he was away a good deal and spent time with his friends, that he had to make a good impression; that it sometimes cost him as much as $50 to $75 an evening to entertain his friends; and then we spoke further. I said that I expected to be very lonely in Albuquerque; and Ethel said that I would make friends; that after a while I would probably meet other people there from New York."

According to Ruth, Ethel continued in this role through September 1945. "Ethel was typing the notes and David was helping her when she couldn't make out his handwriting and explained the technical terms and spelled them out for her, and Julius and I helped her with the phraseology when it got a little too lengthy, wordy." However, things changed in 1946 when, according to Ruth, "Julius and Ethel were going away and they wanted us to stay in their apartment in case any important mail or telephone calls were to be received." At this point, the Kilsheimer led Ruth to testify about a mahogany console table that was designed to be used, with the addition of a lamp, to microfilm Ethel's typed notes.

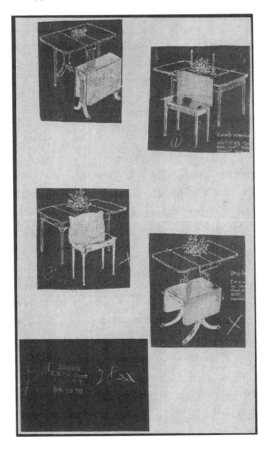

A picture of the same kind of console table used by the Rosenbergs admitted at trial

Ruth subsequently testified about her and David's plans to get out of the country following the 1950 arrest of Gold. "[Julius Rosenberg] gave my husband a package wrapped in brown paper and he said it was $4,000, that there would be more money available in Mexico when we got there. … He told us that we would have to leave sooner than expected, that they were closing in and getting ready to make an arrest...I asked him what he was doing. He said he was going too, that he would not leave at the same time, and he would meet us in Mexico. We would see him there, and I asked him what Ethel thought about it and he said Ethel didn't like the idea of it herself but she realized it was necessary and they were going to go."

Ruth also testified about a strange visit she had from Ethel after David was arrested. "Ethel came with pie for me and gifts for my son, and after we talked in my mother-in-law's house for a few minutes she asked me would I please go out and walk with her. We walked around the block several times and she said her counsel advised her to see me personally and get assurances from me that David would not talk. She said it would only be a matter of a couple of years, and in the long run we would be better off; that Julius had been picked up by the FBI for questioning. He said he was innocent and that he had been released; that she had no doubt that he would probably be picked up again. He would continue to say he was innocent. That if David said he was innocent and Julius said he was innocent, it would strengthen their position; everybody would stand a better chance, and she said do you think it is a dirty shame for David to take the blame and sit for two?"

Harry Gold came to the stand after Ruth and proved to be a star witness for the prosecution. He detailed how he had spied for Russia for 15 years and had even met Anatoli Yakovlev, the Soviet General Counsel and the head of Soviet spy networks in America. He recalled, "Yakovlev was about twenty-eight or thirty years of age at the time I knew him. He was about 5 feet 9 inches in height; had a medium build, which tended toward the slender. He had dark or dark brown hair and there was a lock of it that kept falling over his forehead, which he would brush back continually. He had a rather long nose and a fair complexion, dark eyes. He walked with somewhat of a stoop..."

Yakovlev

He then testified about the meetings the spies held, saying, "[I]f we were just going to discuss the possibility of obtaining certain types of information, the hazards involved, just how much information should be obtained and just what source was needed, then a rather long meeting was scheduled. If I was going to actually get information, very usually a brief meeting was scheduled, the idea being to minimize the time of detection when information would be passed from the American to me. In addition to this I made payments of sums of money to some of the people whom I regularly contacted and always I wrote reports detailing everything that happened at every meeting with these people; and these reports I turned over to Yakovlev. ... The money was given to me by Yakovlev... This is how it worked: We had an arrangement not only for regular meetings but we had an arrangement for alternate meetings, should one of the regular ones not take place, and then in addition to that we had an arrangement for an emergency meeting. This emergency meeting was a one-way affair. A system was set up whereby Yakovlev could get in touch with me if he wanted me quickly. But I couldn't get in touch with him because I didn't know where. Yakovlev told me that in this way the chain was cut in two places. The person from whom I got the information in America did not know me by my true name, nor did he know where I lived, nor could he get in touch with me and I couldn't get in touch with Yakovlev. Yakovlev said this was a good thing. ... I would take the information and put it between the folds of a newspaper and Yakovlev and I would exchange the newspapers. The one that I got was just a newspaper. The one that he got had the information between the folds, the information usually being in some sort of an enclosure."

Of course, Gold's most significant testimony was about one special trip he made: "Yakovlev then gave me a piece of paper; it was onionskin paper, and on it was typed the following: First, the name 'Greenglass,' just 'Greenglass.' Then a number [on] 'High Street'; all that I can recall about the number is . . . it was a low number and . . . the second figure was '0' and the last figure was either 5, 7 or 9; then underneath was 'Albuquerque, New Mexico.' The last thing that was on the paper was 'Recognition signal. I come from Julius.'"

Winding up the prosecution's witness list was Elizabeth Bentley, a romantic figure and media darling then writing memoirs about her life as a Soviet spy. She was followed by Ben Schneider, who ran the small photo shop that the Rosenbergs went to for the 1950 passport photos. The prosecution offered his testimony as proof that Julius and Ethel were planning to flee the country ahead of being arrested.

A picture of Schneider's photo shop introduced at trial

Following Schneider's testimony, the prosecution rested.

Chapter 10: Rosenberg Responded

"Saypol continued his cross-examination of Julius Rosenberg by reciting the names of a number of various persons and asking Rosenberg whether he knew them, to which Rosenberg responded affirmatively for some, negatively for others. When his response was affirmative, Saypol then demanded to know when and where he had met the person, how often he saw the person and, in some instances, whether they exchanged Christmas cards and whether he had met the person at Communist meetings. All the defense attorneys rose to protest that Saypol was asking Rosenberg about matters on which no testimony had been taken or proofs submitted. In effect, they were objecting that Saypol was being permitted to testify in the presence of the jury to unproven matters..... ... These 'questions' constituted uncorroborated testimony by Saypol, and by no other witness, and their effect on the jurors, as he surely knew, would be to make it appear to them that the events described by Saypol in his questions actually occurred and that the witness was being repeatedly evasive. In spite of vigorous objections and motions for mistrials by the defense, Kaufman did not disallow the prosecutor's charge-laden statements in the guise of questions." – Emily Alman, *Exoneration*

The defense surprised the court by calling only two witnesses: Julius and Ethel Rosenberg themselves. Sobell refused to testify.

Julius went first, and when he was asked by the judge about his "preferences of economic systems between Russia and the United States," he answered, "First of all, I am not an expert on matters on different economic systems, but in my normal social intercourse with my friends we discussed matters like that. And I believe there are merits in both systems, I mean from what I have been able to read and ascertain. ... At that time, what I believed at that time I still believe today. In the first place, I heartily approve our system of justice as performed in this country, Anglo-Saxon jurisprudence. I am in favor, heartily in favor, of our Constitution and Bill of Rights and I owe my allegiance to my country at all times...and in discussing the merits of other forms of governments, I discussed that with my friends on the basis of the performance of what they accomplished, and I felt that the Soviet Government has improved the lot of the underdog there, has made a lot of progress in eliminating illiteracy, has done a lot of reconstruction work and built up a lot of resources, and at the same time I felt that they contributed a major share in destroying the Hitler beast who killed six million of my co-religionists and I feel emotional about that thing. ... I would like to state that my personal opinions are that the people of every country should decide by themselves what kind of government they want. If the English want a king, it is their business. If the Russians want communism, it is their business. If the Americans want our form of government, it is our business. I feel that the majority of people should decide for themselves what kind of government they want."

When Rosenberg claimed that David Greenglass had approached him and asked him for $2,000, Judge Kaufman asked him, "And you can't think of any reason whatsoever, can you, why David Greenglass would, of all the people he knew, his brother, all the other members of his family, single you out, as he did apparently and as you say he did, and say that you would be sorry unless you gave him the money?" Rosenberg replied, "Well, he knew that I owed--he had an idea that I owed him money from the business, and I guess that is why he figured he wanted to get money from me."

In response to further questions, Rosenberg went into great detail about his initial questioning by the FBI. "[T]here was a Mr. Norton in the room sitting at a desk with a pad in front of him, and Mr. Harrington sat on the other side of the table. I sat down on the front side of the table and another member of the FBI came in and sat behind, and they started asking questions about what I knew about David Greenglass. First they tried to get my background, what relations I had with him. I gave them my school background, work background and I told them whatever I knew about David Greenglass' education and his work background. ...I told them, and at that point they said to me--they questioned me and tried to focus my attention to, as I notice now, certain dates in the overt acts listed in this indictment. They asked me questions concerning when David Greenglass came in on furlough. I didn't remember. I helped them as much as I could in what I could remember. At one point in the discussion, I would say it was about two hours after I was there, they said to me, 'Do you know that your brother-in-law said you told him to supply information for Russia?' So I said, 'That couldn't be so.' So I said, 'Where is David Greenglass?' I didn't know where he was because I knew he was taken in custody. They wouldn't tell me. I said, 'Will you bring him here and let him tell me that to my face?' And they said, 'What if we bring him here, what will you do?' 'I will call him a liar to his face because that is not so.' And I said, 'Look, gentlemen, at first you asked me to come down an d get some information concerning David Greenglass. Now you are trying to implicate me in something. I would like to see a lawyer! Well, at this point, Mr. Norton said, 'Oh, we are not accusing you of anything. We are just trying to help you.' I said, 'I would like to get in touch with the lawyer for the Federation of Architects and Engineers.' I asked the FBI to please call him. Well, at this point Mr. Norton said, 'Have a smoke, have a piece of gum. Would you like something to eat?' And the language he used in his actions were what the fellows at West Street would call conning--and we discussed around the point. Mr. Norton asked me again, 'Did you ask David Greenglass to turn over information for the Russians?' And I said, 'No.' I denied it. And then we discussed again what periods of time David Greenglass came in. I didn't recall too well and I kept on asking Mr. Norton, 'I want to get in touch with my lawyer.' Finally, some time after lunch, it was probably between 10 and 1, my wife reached me at the FBI office and I told her that the FBI is making some foolish accusations, to please...[I called my attorney and] I told him I was down at the FBI, and he said, 'Are you under arrest?' I said, 'I don't know.' He said, 'Ask the FBI if you are under arrest.' And I asked Mr. Norton, 'Am I under arrest?' He said, 'No.' Then he said, 'Pick yourself up and come down to our office,' and I said, 'Good-bye, gentlemen,' and I left the FBI office."

While discussing how he first came to get in touch with Elitcher, Rosenberg claimed, "I was [in Washington D.C.] alone and I was lonesome and I looked up in the telephone book for Mr. Elitcher's number, and I called him one evening. ... I thought of a couple of people's names who might be in Washington; I remembered the incident at the swimming pool at that time, that Elitcher was in Washington, and perhaps he had a telephone. ... I said something to the effect: 'I am in town; can I come over to see you.' ...he says, 'Come over.'" When the question soon arose as to the men's mutual involvement in the Young Communist League, Rosenberg reacted swiftly, saying, 'I would like to state, on any answer I made on this questions, I don't intend to waive any part of my right of self-incrimination, and if Mr. Saypol is referring to the Young Communist League or the Communist Party, I will not answer any question on it."

Later, Saypol asked Rosenberg about the console table Ruth Greenglass had mentioned. He replied that he had purchased it from Macy's, adding, "I have asked my attorneys to have the Macy's people go through their records and files, and I am sure if the Government request them they will find a sales slip with my signature on it, when I signed in Macy's in 1944 or '45, for that console table, and I believe I bought something else at that time, too. It was shipped to my house. ... I had to pay cash. ... I had to give him the money, and there was--I had to have some notation like a receipt, that I paid the money. I believe the salesman brought over one of these folding booklets, and I signed one of these folding booklets. It was delivered. It was too big for me to take with me. Your Honor, I have requested my attorneys to find that receipt. And my attorneys told me that Macy's cannot find the receipt unless I gave them a number or copy of receipt that I had, because it is filed by number. Now, I feel that if somebody looks through all the numbers through all those years, they will find one for Julius Rosenberg, and it is worth finding if it is such an important issue."

When he was asked about the passport photographs he was said to have purchased, Rosenberg gave an unusual reply, saying, "Well, when I walk with the children, many times with my wife, we would step in; we would have--we would pass a man on the street with one of those box cameras and we would take some pictures. We would step into a place and take some pictures and the pictures we like, we keep. Just--if you take pictures, you just go in, take some pictures, snapshots." He claimed not to have any recollection of any other business.

Ironically, Ethel Rosenberg may have done more to condemn herself than any witness against her. Instead of appearing to be the docile, kindly wife that the jury expected, she came across as something of a hardened shrew who might very well betray her country. That is not to say she did not try to appear fragile; in fact, part of her defense was that she was too feeble to have done the things she was accused of doing. However, when asked about how she managed her home in such a condition, she admitted, "[I had hired help] on occasion for brief periods. I know that when I came from the hospital after the birth of the first child I had some help for the first month, and then upon the time that the second child arrived, I had help for about two months, and there was a period when I was ill and that started about November 1944, I had to have help, right up to about the spring of 1945. ...[I]t so happens that I have had a spinal curvature since I was about thirteen and every once in a while that has given me some trouble, and at that time it began to kick up again. And occasionally I have to get into bed and nurse a severe backache. Through the bargain, I developed a case of low blood pressure, and that used to give me dizzy spells, sometimes to the point where I almost fainted. I also had very severe headaches, and it finally got so bad that I went to visit my doctor. Doctor Max Lionel Hart of Rego Park, Long Island. ...I used to go for iron injections once or twice a week at least once a week, and very often twice a week regularly."

Ethel added that she also had a sickly child whose care took up much of her time: "The condition of my child was very poor. I had had a very difficult time ever since his birth, I mean, with him. He was given to severe colds and sore throat with high fever. It wasn't the usual thing of where a baby gets sick occasionally. It was practically every week in and week out. By the time he was a year and a half old, that winter was extremely severe."

Ethel maintained that they had purchased the console in question from Macy's because "we had decided that we really needed a decent piece of furniture, at least a table, and so we did decide to make that expenditure. It was about $20 or $21. I remember that."

She also testified that she did not even know that her brother was working on the Manhattan

Project, and that they never discussed any plan to pass information to anyone else. Moreover, she adamantly denied that she had ever typed up any notes about the bomb.

What Ethel did affirm was her brother's demand for money. She insisted, "Well, the first time he said that Davey had demanded $2,000 from him and had seemed pretty upset, and that when my husband told him that he had no such amount of money, he couldn't raise any such money for him, he said, 'Well, could you at least do me another favor? Could you at least find out if your doctor will give me a vaccination certificate?' ... I don't recall my husband telling me anything of any reason for it. Except that Dave said that he was in a jam, he was in some trouble. ... I said to my husband, 'Well, doesn't he know the kind of financial situation we are in? Didn't you tell him you can't give him money like that?' ... this time my husband told me that Davey really must be in some very serious trouble, that he was extremely nervous and agitated and that he began to talk wildly, threatened that he would be sorry if he didn't--my husband said that David threatened him, that he, my husband, would be sorry if that money wasn't forthcoming. Well, I told my husband that I thought I should call the house and find out if everything is all right, and my husband said, 'Well, the only thing is, Dave may be working, he may not even be home and I have no way of knowing just how much of this Ruthie knows about...'"

Ethel went on to claim that any film developing equipment that the FBI found in her home must have been based on her husband's brief interest in photography. However, when she was questioned about their trip to have passport photos taken, she became confused. "We, as I tried to explain, my older child was interested in machines, among other things. We, it was our wont to go for walks with them and to stop and look at anything of interest, anything that might be of interest to the children, and very often, as we took these walks, the older child particularly would ask, 'Oh, come, let's go in here and get our pictures taken.' That is--I think kids generally do that kind of thing. Oh, several times. We happen to be what you would call 'snapshot hounds' and that bunch of pictures that you saw there doesn't nearly represent all the snapshots and all the photos that we have had made of ourselves and the children all through our lives. It may have been that time. I am really not sure. There were so many frequent occasions when we dropped into these places. Well, I can't say what I don't recall and I really don't recall specifically."

Ethel did not deny helping David Greenglass join the Communist Party; instead, she invoked her Fifth Amendment right against self-incrimination and refused to answer. This began something of a slide downward for her testimony, leading to the following exchange (during which she admitted to asking Ruth how David was "standing up in jail"):

SAYPOL: You mean, was he talking about you and your husband? Is that what you meant when you asked that?

ETHEL ROSENBERG: Of course not.

SAYPOL: Did you talk at that time about the possibility that perhaps Davey was going to implicate you in this?

ETHEL ROSENBERG: Well, we did recall that the FBI had mentioned, had spoken to my husband in terms of my brother having implicated us, but frankly we didn't believe them.

…

SAYPOL: How would that incriminate you, if you are innocent?

ETHEL ROSENBERG: As long as I had any idea that there might be a chance for me to be incriminated I had the right to use that privilege. …if I used the privilege of self-incrimination at that time, I must have felt that perhaps there might be something that might incriminate me in answering.

SAYPOL: As a matter of fact, at that time you didn't know how much the FBI knew about you and so you weren't taking any chances; isn't that it?

ETHEL ROSENBERG: I was using--I didn't know what the FBI knew or didn't know.

SAYPOL: Of course you didn't, so you weren't taking any chance in implicating yourself or your husband?

At this point, Bloch rose and objected vehemently to the line of questioning, going as far as to ask for a mistrial, which the Court denied. Ethel continued, "Well, if I answered that I didn't want to answer the question on the grounds that it might incriminate me, I must have had a reason to think that it might incriminate me. … He advised me as to my rights, but he also advised me it was entirely up to me to decide, on the basis of what the question was, whether or not I thought any answer might incriminate me, and I so used that right. I can't recall right now what my reasons were at that time for using that right. I said before and I say again, if I used that right, then I must have had some reason or other. I cannot recall right now what that reason might or might not have been, depending on the different questions I was asked..."

As Emily Alman would note in *Exoneration*, "Bloch's examination of Ethel Rosenberg elicited the same responses as her husband had given. In his cross-examination, Saypol attacked Ethel Rosenberg's credibility on the grounds that at the grand jury hearings in the previous year she had declined to answer a number of questions by citing the privilege against self-incrimination, while at the trial she chose to answer some of these questions directly. Bloch objected, but Judge Kaufman upheld Saypol, telling the jurors that Ethel Rosenberg's decision to answer Saypol's questions directly rather than decline to answer them as she had the previous year at the grand jury hearing should be weighed by the jurors in evaluating her credibility. Bloch, as it turned out, was right in his objection. Six years after the trial, the Supreme Court, in *Grunewald v. United*

States, ruled that it violated the Constitutional rights of defendants for prosecutors to use a defendant's access to Fifth Amendment protections at grand jury hearings to attack the defendant's credibility at a jury trial. To allow such a prosecutorial tactic, the Court ruled, would be tantamount to nullifying the protective purpose of the Fifth Amendment."

Chapter 11: Tangible and Circumstantial Evidence

"In making his charge to the jury, Judge Kaufman had to deal with the same problem the prosecution and the defense faced at the trial: he would be unable to lay out each side's tangible and circumstantial evidence, and their opposite interpretations of the testimony. He would, instead, as the prosecution had done, rely on history-as-evidence, express the crime as a Cold War event, describe the times as a clash of ideologies and nations, and accept the prosecution's descriptions of the defendants' motivations. ... Because 'of the development of highly destructive weapons,' he told the jurors, the nation must guard against spying on the secrets of our defense, whether such spying is carried on through agents of foreign powers or through our own nationals who prefer to help a foreign power. The judge pointed out that the mere allegation of the defendants' guilt by the prosecution was not to be taken as proof of guilt. ... He laid out the obligations of the jurors to deliberate without bias, and to take into account the self-interest a witness might have in giving his or her testimony, the credibility of accomplice testimony, the necessity of avoiding inferences of guilt in respect to Sobell for not taking the stand, likewise for defendants who invoked the Fifth Amendment privilege against self-incrimination...." – Emily Alman, *Exoneration*

Bloch began his closing summation by praising the jury, no doubt trying to get them on his side by saying, "The fear that an impartial jury could not be secured was particularly important in this type of case. Now, all of you are New Yorkers or you come from the environs of New York. We are a pretty sophisticated people. People can't put thing over on us very easily."

He then moved on to addressing the prejudices he knew that came with: "We are fairly wise in the ways of the world and the ways of people and we all know that there is not a person in this world who hasn't some prejudice, and you would be inhuman if you didn't have some prejudice. But we ask you now as we asked you before, please don't decide this case because you may have some bias or some prejudice against some political philosophy. If you want to convict these defendants because you think that they are Communists and you don't like communism and you don't like any member of the Communist Party, then, ladies and gentlemen, I can sit down now and there is absolutely no use in my talking. There was no use in going through this whole rigmarole of a three weeks' trial. That is not the crime. But believe me, ladies and gentlemen, I am not here, other defense counsel are not here as attorneys for the Communist Party and we are not here as attorneys for the Soviet Union. ... We are representing Julius and Ethel Rosenberg, two American citizens, who come to you as American citizens, charged with a specific crime, and ask you to judge them the way you would want to be judged if you were sitting over there before twelve other jurors..."

Bloch then moved on to criticizing David Greenglass, telling the jurors, "But one thing I think you do know, that any man who will testify against his own blood and flesh, his own sister, is repulsive, is revolting, who violates every code that any civilization has ever lived by. He is the lowest of the lowest animals that I have ever seen, and if you are honest with yourself, you will admit that he is lowest than the lowest animal that you have ever seen."

Bloch was nearly as harsh when talking about Ruth: "She walked out and put her sister-in-law in. It was a deal that the Greenglasses planned and made for themselves, and they made it--they may not have made it by express agreement with the Government, and I don't think the Government would countenance anything like that, but tell me do actions speak louder than words? Is the proof of the pudding in the eating? Is Ruth Greenglass a defendant here?"

Bloch went on to portray the Rosenbergs as poor, simple, hard-working people: What kind of man was [Julius Rosenberg]? Is this a Costello? Is this your concept of a racketeer? Is this your concept of a pay-off man, a man who lived in a Knickerbocker Village apartment at $45 a month, and finally his rent was raised after many, many years, was raised to $51 a month, whose wife did scrubbing and cleaning and who had two kids, and they had a terrible struggle and they had to go and borrow money, and he scraped together $1,000 in May 1950 to buy stock in the Pitt Machine Company, and he had to give notes for $4,500 for the balance of the purchase price; tell me, does that square with your idea of a pay-off man? ... Now, look at that terrible spy (pointing to the defendant Ethel Rosenberg). Look at that terrible spy and compare her to Ruthie Greenglass, who came here all dolled up, arrogant, smart, cute, eager-beaver, like a phonograph record. ... [Ethel] wanted to help [David Greenglass]. That is human. Can we condemn every member of a family who wants to stick to another member of the family? What is so terrible? Wouldn't you do it, and wouldn't I do it?"

Wrapping up his remarks, Bloch concluded, "I told you at the beginning and I tell you now that we don't come to you in this kind of charge looking for sympathy. Believe me, ladies and gentlemen, there is plenty of room here for a lawyer to try to harp on your emotions, especially so far as Ethel Rosenberg is concerned; a mother, she has two children, her husband is under arrest. No, because if these people are guilty of that crime they deserve no sympathy. No, we want you to decide this case with your minds, not with your hearts, with your minds. . . . I say that if you do that, you can come to no other conclusion than that these defendants are innocent and you are going to show to the world that in America a man can get a fair trial."

In rising for his summation, Saypol pointed out, "All of the partners and employees of the firm do not do the same thing at the same time. While one partner talks to a customer, another may be negotiating with another prospect. . . . Each act by each party, by each employer in the court of business is an act performed for the benefit of the firm and for the benefit of his fellows. Imagine a wheel. In the center of the wheel, Rosenberg, reaching out like the tentacles of an octopus. Rosenberg to David Greenglass. Ethel Rosenberg, Ruth Greenglass; Rosenberg to Harry Gold;

Rosenberg, Yakovlev. Information obtained, supplied. Rosenberg, Sobell, Elitcher--always the objective in the center coming from all the legs, all the tentacles going to the one center, solely for the one object: The benefit of Soviet Russia. The sources, Government sources, Los Alamos, atomic information. Sobell, Elitcher, information from the Navy, relating particularly to gunfire control; always secret, always classified, always of advantage to a foreign government."

He also addressed the reliability of David Greenglass and Harry Gold as witnesses, casting them as men with nothing to gain by testifying: "There is no condonation for the activities of the Greenglasses in 1944 and 1945. David Greenglass is a confessed member of the Rosenberg espionage ring. . . By his own plea of guilty, by his own voluntary act, without weaving a web of lies in an attempt to deceive you, he has made himself liable to the death penalty, too. The spurious defense that Greenglass, or the Greenglasses, in order to satisfy a business grudge, a business dispute against the Rosenbergs, has concocted a story about espionage, making himself liable to the capital penalty by his plea of guilty because of the business disagreement, is as much of a concoction as the story of the defendants that Greenglass went to his worst enemy, Julius Rosenberg, for help when he wanted to flee the country. ... As far as Gold is concerned, the die has already been cast. The charges against him have already been disposed of. He has been sentenced to thirty years, the maximum term of imprisonment. He can gain nothing from testifying as he did in this courtroom except the initial relief, the moral satisfaction in his soul of having told the truth and tried to make amends. Harry Gold, who furnished the absolute corroboration of the testimony of the Greenglasses, forged the necessary link in the chain that points indisputably to the guilt of the Rosenbergs. Not one question was asked of him by any defendant on cross-examination."

Finally, Saypol fell back on the biggest issue in America at that time: the fear of Communism. "Ladies and gentlemen, you have heard statements of defense counsel here concerning the injection of communism in this case. I repeat again, these defendants are not on trial for being Communists. I don't want you to convict them merely because of their Communist activity. Communism, as the testimony has demonstrated, has a very definite place in this case because it is the Communist ideology which teaches worship and devotion to the Soviet Union over our own government. It has provided the motive and inspiration for these people to do the terrible things which have been proven against them. It is this adherence and devotion which makes clear their intent and motivation in carrying out this conspiracy to commit espionage. We ask you to sustain the charge of the grand jury in a verdict of guilty against each of these three defendants, on one basis and one basis alone; the evidence produced in this courtroom as to their guilt of the crime of conspiracy to commit espionage; that proof as to each defendant has been overwhelming. The guilt of each one has been established beyond any peradventure of doubt. I am a firm believer in the American jury system. I have confidence in the perception of the jury of twelve intelligent American citizens. I am confident that you will render the only verdict possible on the evidence presented before you in this courtroom--that of guilty as charged by the grand jury as to each of these three defendants."

At this point, Judge Kaufman charged the jury with instructions before sending them on their way, and they debated only a few hours before returning a verdict of guilty against all three defendants. It then fell to Kaufman to pass sentence, which he did by giving Sobell 30 years in prison and ordering Julius and Ethel Rosenberg executed. He said, "Citizens of this country who betray their fellow-countrymen can be under none of the delusions about the benignity of Soviet power that they might have been prior to World War II. The nature of Russian terrorism is now self-evident. Idealism as a rational dissolves.... I consider your crime worse than murder. ...I believe your conduct in putting into the hands of the Russians the A-bomb years before our best scientists predicted Russia would perfect the bomb has already caused, in my opinion, the Communist aggression in Korea, with the resultant casualties exceeding 50,000 and who knows but that millions more of innocent people may pay the price of your treason. Indeed, by your betrayal you undoubtedly have altered the course of history to the disadvantage of our country. No one can say that we do not live in a constant state of tension. We have evidence of your treachery all around us every day--for the civilian defense activities throughout the nation are aimed at preparing us for an atom bomb attack. Nor can it be said in mitigation of the offense that the power which set the conspiracy in motion and profited from it was not openly hostile to the United States at the time of the conspiracy. ... In the light of this, I can only conclude that the defendants entered into this most serious conspiracy against their country with full realization of its implications..."

Though the verdict was rendered and the sentence passed, the case was far from over. Emanuel Bloch devoted the next two years of his life to trying to save the Rosenbergs from the chair; he cared for their sons, filed appeal after appeal, and even stood outside the White House gate begging to appeal to President Eisenhower. President Eisenhower refused to commute the sentence, saying, "I can only say that, by immeasurably increasing the chances of atomic war, the Rosenbergs may have condemned to death tens of millions of innocent people all over the world. The execution of two human beings is a grave matter. But even graver is the thought of the millions of dead whose deaths may be directly attributable to what these spies have done."

Ultimately, the case landed before the Supreme Court, which observed, "The existence of our power was clear, and so also, we think, was the necessity for its exercise. Yet it was urged at argument that the Court, as a matter of discretion if not of power, should refrain from immediately deciding the merits of the issue which had been preserved by the stay. Indeed, the reasons for refusing, as matters of practice, to vacate stays issued by single Justices are obvious enough. Ordinarily the stays of individual Justices should stand until the grounds upon which they have issued can be reviewed through regular appellate processes. ... This Court has the responsibility to supervise the administration of criminal justice by the federal judiciary. This includes the duty to see that the laws are not only enforced by fair proceedings, but also that the punishments prescribed by the laws are enforced with a reasonable degree of promptness and certainty. The stay which had been issued promised many more months of litigation in a case which had otherwise run its full course. The question preserved for adjudication by the stay was entirely legal; there was no need to resort to the fact finding processes of the District Court; it was a question of statutory construction which this Court was equipped to answer. We decided that a proper administration of the laws required the Court to consider that question forthwith. … We need not reiterate here what has been said in those opinions. It is enough to add that, in our view, the ultimate decision was clear."

While four justices voted for a stay, five were against, so the executions proceeded as planned on June 19, 1953. The couple insisted they were innocent until the day they died, with Julius characterizing his fate as a byproduct of the Smith Act's ban of the Communist Party in the country. Julius asserted that Judge Kaufman's ruling was merely another way of saying, "Alleged Communists or pro-Communists are better off dead."

In the wake of the executions, the British paper *The Times* reported, "The bodies had been brought from Sing Sing prison by the national 'Rosenberg committee' which undertook the funeral arrangements, and an all-night vigil was held in one of the largest mortuary chapels in Brooklyn. Many hundreds of people filed past the biers. Most of them clearly regarded the Rosenbergs as martyred heroes and more than 500 mourners attended to-day's services, while a crowd estimated at 10,000 stood outside in burning heat. Mr. Bloch [their counsel], who delivered one of the main orations, bitterly exclaimed that America was 'living under the heel of a military dictator garbed in civilian attire': the Rosenbergs were 'sweet. tender. and intelligent' and the course they took was one of 'courage and heroism.'"

Over 60 years after Julius and Ethel Rosenberg were executed, historians continue to analyze the case, and such studies have been bolstered by revelations that came decades later. David Greenglass would later admit during an interview with the *New York Times* that it was his own wife who had typed up incriminating notes, not his sister Ethel: "I frankly think my wife did the typing, but I don't remember. My wife is more important to me than my sister. Or my mother or my father, O.K.? And she was the mother of my children." When the grand jury proceedings were declassified, scholars immediately found a similar discrepancy between what Ruth said before the grand jury and at trial; she had admitted writing notes to the grand jury and subsequently attributed it to Ethel at trial.

While there is still plenty of debate over Ethel's culpability, most historians devote energy to trying to determine the extent of Julius' spying instead of seeking to exonerate him entirely. Soviet premier Nikita Khrushchev would later claim while he "cannot specifically say what kind of help the Rosenbergs provided us," they "had provided very significant help in accelerating the production of our atomic bomb."

Sobell would not admit to being a Soviet spy until he was in his 90s, but he continued to insist that while Julius was a spy, he had not provided particularly important information on nuclear weapons to the Soviets. He also claimed Ethel knew about the espionage but was not an active participant in it.

Online Resources

Other books about 20th century American history by Charles River Editors

Other books about Alger Hiss on Amazon

Other books about the Rosenbergs on Amazon

Bibliography

Alman, Emily A. and David. Exoneration: The Trial of Julius and Ethel Rosenberg and Morton Sobell – Prosecutorial deceptions, suborned perjuries, anti-Semitism, and precedent for today's unconstitutional trials. Green Elms Press, 2010. ISBN 978-0-9779058-3-6 or ISBN 0-9779058-3-7.

Chambers, Whittaker (1952). *Witness*. Random House.

Cook, Fred J (1957). *The Unfinished Story of Alger Hiss*. New York: William Morrow.

Cooke, Alistair (1950). *A Generation on Trial: USA v. Alger Hiss*. Greenwood Press.

Feklisov, Aleksandr, and Kostin, Sergei. The Man Behind the Rosenbergs. Enigma Books, 2003. ISBN 978-1-929631-24-7.

Hartshorn, Lewis. *Alger Hiss, Whittaker Chambers and the Case That Ignited McCarthyism*. Jefferson, North Carolina: McFarland, 2013.

Hiss, Alger (1957). *In the Court of Public Opinion*. Harper Collins.

   (1988). *Recollections of a Life*. Little Brown & Co.

Hornblum, Allen M. The Invisible Harry Gold: The Man Who Gave the Soviets the Atom Bomb, Yale University Press 2010. ISBN 0-300-15676-6.

Jacoby, Susan (2009). *Alger Hiss and the Battle for History*. New Haven: Yale University Press.

Meeropol, Robert and Michael. We Are Your Sons, The Legacy of Ethel and Julius Rosenberg. University of Illinois Press, 1986. [chapter 15 is a detailed refutation of Radosh and Milton's scholarship.] ISBN 0-252-01263-1.

Meeropol, Michael, ed. The Rosenberg Letters: A Complete Edition of the Prison Correspondence of Julius and Ethel Rosenberg NY, Garland Publishing, 1994 ISBN 0-8240-5948-4

Meeropol, Robert Meeropol. An Execution in the Family: One Son's Journey. St. Martin's Press, 2003. ISBN 0-312-30637-7.

Nason, Tema. Ethel: The Fictional Autobiography of Ethel Rosenberg. Delacourt, 1990. ISBN 0-440-21110-7 and by Syracuse, 2002, ISBN 0-8156-0745-8.

Radosh, Ronald and Joyce Milton. The Rosenberg File: A Search for the Truth. Henry Holt (1983). ISBN 0-03-049036-7.

Roberts, Sam. The Brother: The Untold Story of the Rosenberg Case. Random House, 2001. ISBN 0-375-76124-1.

Schneir, Walter. Final Verdict: What Really Happened in the Rosenberg Case, Melville House, 2010. ISBN 1-935554-16-6.

Schneir, Walter. Invitation to an Inquest. Pantheon Books, 1983. ISBN 0-394-71496-2.

Schrecker, Ellen. Many Are the Crimes: McCarthyism in America. Little, Brown and Company, 1998. ISBN 0-316-77470-7.

Smith, John Chalbot (1976). *Alger Hiss: The True Story*. New York, Holt Rinehart Winston.

Swan, Patrick (Editor) (2003). *Alger Hiss, Whittaker Chambers, and the Schism in the American Soul*.

Trahair, Richard C.S. and Robert Miller. Encyclopedia of Cold War Espionage, Spies, and Secret Operations. Enigma Books, 2009. ISBN 978-1-929631-75-9.

Weinstein, Allen (1997). *Perjury: The Hiss-Chambers Case* (2d rev. ed.). Knopf.

Wexley, John. The Judgment of Julius and Ethel Rosenberg. Ballantine Books, 1977. ISBN 0-345-24869-4.

White, G. Edward (2005). *Alger Hiss's Looking-Glass Wars: The Covert Life of a Soviet Spy*. Oxford University Press.

Yalkowsky, Stanley. The Murder of the Rosenbergs. Crucible Publications (July 1990). ISBN 978-0-9620984-2-0.

Made in the USA
Middletown, DE
01 July 2021

43452807R00057